CISTERCIAN FATHERS SERIES: NUMBER FORTY

BERNARD OF CLAIRVAUX

ON THE
SONG OF SONGS IV

CISTERCIAN FATHERS SERIES: NUMBER FORTY

Bernard of Clairvaux
ON THE SONG OF SONGS IV

Translated by
IRENE EDMONDS

Introduction by
JEAN LECLERCQ

Cistercian Publications
Kalamazoo, Michigan 49008
1980

CISTERCIAN FATHERS SERIES

BOARD OF EDITORS

The translation here presented is based on the critical Latin edition prepared by Jean Leclercq, H. M. Rochais and C. H. Talbot, under the sponsorship of the S. Order of Cistercians and published by Editiones Cistercienses, Piazza Tempo di Diana 14, I-00143 Rome.

First published 1980
by
Cistercian Publications Inc.
Kalamazoo, Michigan 49008

Available in Britain, Europe, and the Commonwealth (except Canada) from A. R. Mowbray & Co Ltd St Thomas House Becket Street Oxford OX1 1SJ

Library of Congress Cataloging in Publication Data (Revised)
Bernard de Clairvaux, Saint, 1091?–1153.
   On the Song of Songs.

   (The Works of Bernard of Clairvaux, v. 2, 3, 4)
(Cistercian Fathers series, no. 4, 7, 31, 40)
   Vols. (2–4) have imprints Kalamazoo, Mich.,
Cistercian Publications.
   1. Bible. O.T. Song of Solomon—Sermons. 2. Sermons,
Latin—Translations into English. 3. Sermons,
English—Translations from Latin. I. Title.
II. Series: Bernard de Clairvaux, Saint, 1091?–1153.
Works. English. 1970. v. 2 [etc.]
BX890.B5 1970, vol. 2, etc. [BS1485] 230'.2s [223'.9'073]
ISBN 0-87907-104-4   73-168262

*Book design by Gale Akins. Typeset at Humble Hills Graphics, Kalamazoo
Printed in the United States of America*

With respect and appreciation
the editors of Cistercian Publications
dedicate this volume

to the memory of

SISTER PENELOPE LAWSON csmv
1890–1977

who did so much to keep alive the
writings of the medieval spiritual fathers

CONTENTS

THE MAKING OF A MASTERPIECE

THE DOCTRINE taught in the Sermons on the Song of Songs has already been presented in the Introductions to volumes one and three of the present translation. In the beginning of volume two, the literary form of this work has been described: a series of treatises in the form of sermons, but sermons which have not been presented verbally before an audience; they have been 'dictated' (*dictare*) to a secretary, then reproduced (*transcribere*) in several copies with a view to being 'edited' (*edere*).[1] They are in contrast to another whole part of Bernard's oratorical work, those sermons that had not been drafted in writing but rather delivered verbally, then 'noted down' by listeners in the form of 'diverse sermons, brief sermons, sentences, parables'. The discovery of these facts has resulted from meticulous research into a manuscript tradition that is exceptionally vast and old. Only a knowledge of the methods of production of written works of the twelfth century—which differ from those of antiquity and those of the period which begins with the thirteenth century—permits us to ascertain these facts. No other expertise in literary history—not even that having Holy Scripture as its object, including the synoptic Gospels in their relationships with their possible common source[2]—authorizes one to judge facts that are peculiar to the time of St Bernard and, more specifically, to himself and his milieu.

The Sermons on the Song of Songs constitute not only a masterpiece of theology; they are also a literary masterpiece—one of the greatest masterpieces of universal literature—and, no more than any of the others, this one was not produced instantly and effortlessly. It has a long history, which is extremely complex and which has been explained in detail elsewhere.[3] It will suffice here only to recount that which will help the reader better to appreciate the quality of the text he has before him. St Bernard deserves better than a rapid and superficial reading; he should be read with the same care and precision with which he wrote. His entire message of truth is enveloped in beauty, and this is achieved by the numerous refinements he had the genius to invent. They are sometimes so fine and so delicate that they risk eluding us. It is therefore useful to draw attention to them.

When I was asked, in 1947, to undertake a critical edition of all the works of St Bernard, one idea seemed to impose itself: since, unlike the treatises, letters, and sermons—which are all works of a brief and diverse nature—the *Sermons on the Song of Songs* constituted a long work marked by the unity its theme imposed on him, one could suppose that it was homogeneous. It would be enough then to choose some old manuscripts of good provenance and guaranteed quality in order to establish the text. Since the library at Troyes, where we find the greatest number of the old manuscripts originating from the abbey of Clairvaux, possesses two copies of the twelfth-century *Sermons on the Song of Songs,* it seemed natural to begin the work with them. And so I did. It became necessary, little by little, however, to recognize a double truth: on the one hand the textual tradition was much more complex than I had foreseen; on the other hand, these two manuscripts from Clairvaux (designated by the abbreviations Cl and Cl[1]) presented a text which included not only some mistakes by the copyist, but some readings inferior in quality to those of most of the other witnesses.

Ten years of, sometimes agonizing, research, of long trips, of comparisons, of verifications, led to some results that have illustrated not only the stages of the redaction, but also the working methods of St Bernard. It is not therefore fruitless that this lively history of the 'making', so to speak, of the text itself be first recapitulated, before we go on to mention the great beauty that resulted from so much effort.

I. A CONTEMPLATIVE IN HISTORY

The long series of eighty-six *Sermons on the Song of Songs* was not divided by Bernard into 'books' or 'chapters' corresponding to a logical plan established in advance. They were composed as the author found time to spare or various problems he wished to confront, or with an eye to contemporary events on which he wanted to take a stand. Considering the whole manuscript tradition and the chronological data at one's disposal, one can say that St Bernard successively put into circulation the following four groupings:

—Sermons one to twenty-four
—Sermons twenty-four to forty-nine
—Sermons fifty to eighty-three
—Sermons eighty-four to eighty-six.

To the first group it is possible to assign dates that are relatively precise. Sermon One which, like a preface or a prologue, constitutes a veritable Introduction to all that is to follow, was begun after Bernard had returned from a trip to Aquitaine at the end of July 1135. The work was interrupted in December 1136, when Pope Innocent II and the Cardinals summoned him to travel a third time to Italy to put an end to the schism provoked by the anti-pope Anacletus. Bernard had dictated twenty-four sermons.

Upon his return from Italy, during the summer of 1138, he took up his work again. He dictated a new redaction of Sermon Twenty-four, beginning it with an allusion to his third sojourn at Rome and to the schism finally ended. He also modified the rest of the sermon. Sermon Thirty-three was composed before Lent of 1139, and the grouping Twenty-four to Forty-nine was probably completed in 1145.

Sermons Fifty to Eighty-three occupied the following years. Sermons Sixty-five and Sixty-six came in response to a request that Eberwin, Provost of the Premonstratensians of Steinfeld, in the Rhineland, had addressed to Bernard: towards 1144, he invited him there to refute the heretics, the 'cathars', of the region. Sermon Eighty, in which Bernard makes allusion to the doctrine of Gilbert of Poitiers and to the Council of Rheims of 1148, is subsequent to that Council.

During his final years, Bernard worked on Sermons Eighty-four to Eighty-six, the last of which was to remain unfinished when he died on 20 August 1153. Several manuscripts allude, with a discreet emotion, to the uneven and decidedly incomplete character of this 'unfinished symphony'. A contemporary of St Bernard, Gerhoh of Reichersberg, went so far as to declare: 'For many of us your wedding song has turned into a song of mourning.' Throughout the rest of the century, several Cistercians successively endeavored to comment on the Song of Songs, beginning with verse two of the second chapter, where St Bernard had been interrupted, and going to the end of this biblical book. One of them, Geoffrey of Auxerre, succeeded in doing so in a work that is not lacking in merit. By contrast, however, all these attempts only make more appreciable the unique quality of the masterpiece that occupied the last eighteen years of the life of the first Abbot of Clairvaux.

During this period of his life, as previously, Bernard was a busy man. He became even more so in the measure that his reputation spread, that his influence grew, that the foundations of Clairvaux multiplied, and that he found himself more and more involved in the affairs of the Church. Nonetheless, he never ceased to be an artist, dissatisfied with what he had composed, desirous of improving it. Each time he circulated a new group of sermons, therefore, he corrected the text. In his last years, he proceeded with a meticulous revision of all his literary works, including the *Sermons on the Song of Songs*. The result of all this work was that there

came to be, during Bernard's lifetime, two principal redactions of the Sermons: the first extends as far as and includes Sermon Eighty-three. It can be described as follows:
  —first of all, it is incomplete;
  —next, Sermon Twenty-four appears there in its first redaction, which begins with the first words of this verse from the Song of Songs: '*Recti diligunt te*—Those who are righteous love you';
  —moreover, in Sermon Seventy-one, a point of trinitarian theology is the object of a rather brief passage beginning with the word '*Denique*'.
The second, definitive, redaction differs from the first in respect to the following points:
  —it is longer;
  —Sermon Twenty-four is presented there in its second redaction, beginning with '*Hoc demum tertio*—Here I am at last, back for the third time [from Rome]';
  —in Sermon Seventy-one, the passage *Denique* has been replaced by a longer treatment, the first word of which is *Consensio*;
  —finally, at hundreds of points, often of detail, corrections have been introduced; in particular, in Sermon Seventy-one, the adverb *rotunde,* applied to the Trinity, has been replaced by the word *perfecte,* which has the same meaning of 'totality', but expresses it differently.
    The first redaction was preserved in the areas where Cistercian foundations of the filiation of Morimond had spread, toward the east of Champagne. It has therefore been designated by the abbreviation M. The second redaction is best preserved in England; whence the initial A (*Anglica*) by which it is designated. On the continent, the two redactions contaminated one another and gave birth to an intermediate text designated by the initial T, from the words *Textus medius.* Lastly, during the years that followed the death of Bernard, the monks at Clairvaux, with a view to preparing a dossier to obtain his canonization from Rome, proceeded

with a revision of the *Sermons on the Song of Songs*. According to a sort of 'law of the milieu', of which history offers other examples, they arrogated the right to modify his text, often in points of detail. But no one was in a position to improve it. On the contrary, they either made a mess of it or they reintroduced into it from the first redaction certain imperfections which Bernard had remedied in the second. For example, in Sermon Seventy-one, they juxtaposed the two passages *Denique* and *Consensio,* one of which should have replaced the other. This 'Clairvaux redaction', designated by the initial C, is preserved in the two manuscripts originating at Clairvaux which are designated Cl and Cl[1]. They are not even entirely in conformity with one another. Evidently, those who entrusted themselves with this redaction, destined to become the official text, worked in haste and without care, probably because the copyroom or scriptorium of Clairvaux was very busy at the time. We know that the *Vita prima* of St Bernard was subjected to a similar revision, always with the intention of preparing the dossier of canonization.[4]

This liberty appropriated to itself by the milieu in which St Bernard lived astonishes us today. It illustrates the fact that in former times people did not have the same notion of 'literary property' that we have in our day. The monks of Clairvaux, perhaps even the General Chapter of the Cistercian Order, considered the works of St Bernard family property, in the same way as they would the relics of his body and the things which had belonged to him. The monastery of the Visitandines of Annecy acted the same way in the seventeenth century with respect to the writings of St Francis de Sales, and so did the Cistercian monastery of Port-Royal with regard to the *Pensées* of Pascal. In modern times, the most famous example of similar conduct is offered by the manner in which the nuns of the Carmel of Lisieux, and in particular even one of the sisters of St Thérèse, modified the saint's writings. Fortunately, they preserved her original manuscripts, thanks to which it has been possible to restore the authentic text its charm and its vigor. In any case, the intention, considered legitimate in these times and milieux, had been zealous, but the interventions were always awkward.[5] It is not enough to know grammar and the rules of style to be a great writer. When one tinkers with an eminent masterpiece, all that one can do is diminish its quality. Happily, in the case of St Bernard, several English monasteries, even among the Cistercians, maintained enough independence never to permit the degradation of the treasure they had received in its second redaction.

After the death, and then the canonization of St Bernard, no one stopped transcribing his *Sermons on the Song of Songs* according to the different redactions, mixing them, abridging them, commenting on them, drawing up concordances of them, introducing into them subtitles designed to make them easier reading.[6] Equally early and, so it seems, even before he was canonized in 1174, they were translated into French. In this language, as well as in Latin, they exercised an influence on a poet like Chrétien de Troyes, on cycles of tales like that of the Grail, and, moreover, in the domain of the iconography of the Song of Songs and even on the wording of certain charters.[7] Therefore the posthumous history of this masterpiece is as lively as had been its 'making', if one can express it so, during the lifetime of its author. In these sermons are reflected the major concerns and crises of the Church: the reform of monasticism and of the clergy; doctrinal controversies; the schism of Anacletus; the dangers presented by popular heresies. One sees Bernard engaged in action in the service of the Spouse. He travels and he struggles on several fronts at the same time. Yet he never manifests any agitation. In the midst of so many battles, he remains a contemplative, following the example of the man whom Bernard himself proposed as a model: St Gregory the Great, who was composing his homilies on the contemplation of God following the prophet

Ezekiel at the very moment when the barbarians were besieg-
ing the gates of Rome.[8] Of the different affairs of the
Church in which Bernard was involved between the beginning and the end of the *Sermons on the Song of Songs,*
there is one of which he does not speak: the second
crusade. And this silence without doubt helps restore to its
relative importance this event whose place in Bernard's life
certain historians have tended to exaggerate. It was, in
reality, only a parenthesis, late and of short duration.
Certainly, Bernard was grieved by the failure of this enter-
prise, and he would speak of it elsewhere,[9] but he never
lost his peace.

The redaction of the eighty-six *Sermons on the Song of
Songs* was interrupted many times, and at least one of these
interruptions lasted a year and a half. There is no evidence
of this in the style, with the exception of Sermon Twenty-
four in the second redaction, where Bernard explains, with
serenity, the meaning of his recent sojourn in Italy. He does
not linger to give news of it, as he would have of just any
event. He does better: he seeks from this fact and from his
own conduct a meaning, and he finds in the events themselves a stimulus for the contemplation of the mystery of
the Church and of union with God. When death will inter-
rupt him for good, he will only be able to advance to its
ultimate and glorious end, on the way indicated by the final
words, borrowed from St Paul, of the last, unfinished,
sermon: 'Walk as sons of the light . . . '.[10]

II. BEAUTY IN THE SERVICE OF TRUTH

The working methods of St Bernard and of the authors of his
time are known. The different phases are designated by a
precise vocabulary: successively one 'noted down' the ideas
on wax tablets; then one 'dictated' to a secretary (called a
'notary' or a 'scribe') a text that he 'wrote' on parchment. If

he deemed it necessary—and we know that this was the case with St Bernard—the author read or had read aloud to him the written text; then he dictated the corrections. This phase is that of *emendatio*. This operation could be repeated an indefinite number of times. At the end, or at one of the intermediate stages, copies were made according to the *exemplar* thus composed. The text was then put into circula-tion, that is to say, published (*edere*). Thus, during the author's lifetime and after his death, his text did not cease to 'live', that is to say, to be modified, contrary to what came to be the case from the moment when the printing shop fixed the composed text typographically—unless the author presented the printers with a new manuscript of the text or a printed edition to which he had added corrections.

We know that Bernard reworked, once or several times, nearly all his texts. This confers on his 'edited' works a style extremely different from that of the sermons which he delivered without 'dictating' them and having them put in writing. Like St Augustine and the authors of antiquity and of the Middle Ages who had, on the one hand, spoken without writing and, on the other hand, composed without speaking before an audience, Bernard had two styles: a written style and an oral style. His 'literary' style appears in the *Sermons on the Song of Songs* more brilliantly because they were made the object, on his part, of an *emendatio* that extended over a greater number of years.

Why did this man, who was so busy, give himself to so exacting an activity of revision? To this question an initial observation imposes an astonishing response: except in the case of the passage *Denique-Consensio* of Sermon Seventy-one, the corrections of the author do not deal with questions of doctrine. Even in this case, moreover, the new redaction consists in specifying and developing a teaching already given, without modifying the content. The only reason for the changes then can have been to improve the style, in other words, a concern for beauty. This 'aesthetic' of St Bernard involves both theory and practice. Both have been the object of detailed research.[11] At the beginning of volume two of the critical edition of the *Sermons on the Song of Songs,* Christine Mohrmann has deployed her expertise as a philologist in analyzing, in a very technical way, certain of the stylistic processes of St Bernard. It is difficult to treat such a subject without citing numerous examples in Latin. It will be enough here to describe in a general manner the different means by which Bernard endeavored to render even more perfect a first redaction that was already a masterpiece. This will permit us to penetrate a little into his psychology as an author.

Three preoccupations dominated Bernard: precision of vocabulary; grammatical quality; and euphony. The first appears in the choice he made of words to substitute one for the other in improving the first redaction. He preferred then, as the case might be, a more precise, or a more unusual and more refined, word, or one better suited to the context. In doing this, it was often sufficient for him to make only a brief modification, touching on the prefix or beginning of the word, or on the last syllable and the inflexion, sometimes even on a single letter situated at the beginning, at the end, or in the body of the word. In every case, there results from this a new meaning or a new nuance, sometimes subtle, fine, but perceptible to the intelligence and to the ear of the attentive listener. The reasons that may have determined these slight corrections may escape us. They were perhaps imponderable even in Bernard's mind, but they were certainly never lacking. Only a study of the style of the complete works of Bernard will be able to shed light on this problem. This remains to be undertaken, and it has become possible only recently, since the critical edition of the whole has been finished.

The corrections employed for the grammatical constructions are of exactly the same kind as those which touched upon vocabulary. They too were often very slight. They almost always introduced a more refined reading, which is an improvement, enhancing a subtle art. They can be explained only as having been suggested to the author by a first redaction, already correct but capable of being still more perfected. They often touch the tense and the mood of verbs, those action words that give Bernard's style so much vigor. Some pronouns, some prepositions, and some adverbs were inserted when they added a new precision; when they were useless or of little significance, as so easily happens in every language with this kind of word, Bernard suppressed them pitilessly. He wanted his style to be strong and concise.

Finally, the corrections most difficult for us to judge are those that aim at giving the text greater euphony. This word, of Greek origin, comes from the tradition of the ancient Latin grammarians. In the beginning of the Middle Ages, St Isidore of Seville had explained that it means 'The sweetness of the voice', and—in a play on words that Latin permitted—he related this sweetness of 'melody' to that of honey: *melos, mellis.* It comes therefore from the 'ear' and from the 'taste', rather than from the reason. In contrast to those which modify the grammar and vocabulary, these corrections which aim at embellishing the musicality sometimes bear on entire passages. Sometimes they consist only of an inversion of the order of two words. The motive is not always clear to an ear no longer attuned to twelfth century language. One has difficulty imagining how Bernard and his contemporaries pronounced Latin, all the more so in that this pronunciation must have varied from one region to another, as it still does in our day. However, the manuscript tradition, vast and well-established, obliges one to state that these inversions do not result, as one might spontaneously think to be the case, from errors by the copyists. They were intentional. In certain cases, it seems from the order of the words and from the vocabulary and grammar that Bernard may at first have expressed himself as a man accustomed to a romance language. Later he chose what was, so to speak, 'more Latin', or appeared so to him.

The result of all this work was to increase the precision and the conciseness of the discourse. Elliptical formulas are developed and rendered more clear. Redundancies are avoided. Insistences are emphasized. The rhythm of the formulas and the phrases is likewise improved by the combined modification of words, of grammar, of the musicality of the sounds. Some new *jeux de mots* are suggested which are also *jeux de sens;* certain pages thus become veritable fireworks. Obviously, Bernard sought for effect, in order to hold the attention and to charm the ear. He reworked with special care the texts to which, more than to the others, he intended to give a literary character; one of these is in Sermon Twenty-four, where he justifies his intervention in the schism that had divided the Roman Church. Another comes in Sermon Twenty-six with the splendid lament over the death of Gerard. Others occur in passages dealing with controversies or subtle doctrines, like the second half of Sermon Sixty-six against the heretics of the Rhineland, or Sermon Seventy-one on the Trinity. With Bernard, the poet and the artist were at the service of the theologian.

One series of corrections by the author now merits special attention: those passages in which Bernard modified the text of a biblical citation or reminiscence. Two intentions moved him. The first involves rendering a biblical allusion more consistent with the text which was then recognized as having the most value, that of the Vulgate. Bernard had spontaneously cited from memory in an imprecise way. He then made an effort to come closer to the very letter of Scripture. Or else he had cited according to a different version of the Vulgate, following the Fathers of the Church, the Rule of St Benedict, or the liturgy, and then he returned to the Vulgate. Yet a second concern shows itself equally: that of remaining free with respect to the letter. Bernard, so to speak, plays with Scripture. He made it serve his own ends and did not hesitate, if there was good reason, to modify it to fit the precise and harmonious message he wished to communicate. One sometimes has the impression that he was amusing himself, in a way, by seeking 'biblical effects'. One catches a glimpse of his discreet humor and of the smile he wanted to evoke from his reader, surprised by a formula modified in an unexpected way or used in a sense different from that which it has in its original context, or sometimes even contrary to that context. This difference did not escape him, for the normal and easy reading was in the text he wished to modify in order to make it more expressive.[12]

Not being able to cite and to comment upon many of the examples of these corrections by the author—which are innumerable—we must be content here to linger a bit on one of them which has already been mentioned. In Sermon 71.6, describing the absolute unity there is in the Trinity between the Father and the Son, Bernard first used the expression *rotunde unum*. The first of these two words evokes the round, or spherical, form which in the Greek and Latin philosophical tradition symbolized plenitude. 'When we wish to say that a thing is excellent and absolutely perfect, we say that it is round', wrote Cicero, for example. This image dates back to early antiquity; it was in the works of Empedocles, previous to Socrates, then in the works of Plato. The profane Latin writers like Horace and Marcus Aurelius revived it, and among the Latin Fathers and the medieval authors there is no lack of examples.[13] The word 'roundly' therefore possessed a certain nobility; it had in the tradition a precise and technical meaning. The fact that Bernard had spontaneously used it in his first redaction proves that he was acquainted with this notion from the culture of antiquity. Why, in correcting it, did he replace the word *rotunde* by *perfecte*? This word also expresses totality, but in a more abstract way and without the poetic nuance attached to the metaphor of the circle or the sphere. It was this word that was preferred by most of the witnesses of the teaching

authority of the Church. It was therefore the word with
which most of the readers of Bernard's time were familiar.
In order to be understood, it did not suppose any pre-
liminary knowledge of the culture of antiquity. In adopting
it in place of a word more unusual but less familiar, Bernard
gives evidence of pastoral deference, as he did in dictating
again the entire trinitarian discussion of the same Sermon
Seventy-one which began with *Denique.* Bernard was concerned with beauty, but he never sacrificed to it the good of
the faithful and the profit they should draw from his teaching. He avoided making things uselessly difficult. His charity
impelled him to put himself at the service of all without
requiring that they be aware of a philosophical tradition not
bound to the faith of the Church.

Thus the corrections brought by Bernard to bear on his
text render it even more lively. They permit us to be present,
in some way, as he worked. One can almost hear him repeat-
ing to himself, aloud and over and over again, each phrase or
expression, hesitating, weighing, crossing out, as a poet
listens to the verse he has just written, as a composer plays
each of his chords before noting them down definitively.
Hardly ever do the changes affect the meaning, although they
sometimes modify its nuances. These are the corrections
of an artist, of a man of letters and a humanist, demanding of
himself, concerned with many details that are purely aesthetic, constantly improving, even one last time before dying,
the work he is going to leave to posterity.

The art of writing is the art of astonishing. Bernard knew
this. He submitted himself to the demands of the profession.
He sought effect. Yet he almost always did so with a very
great discretion. He avoided the too obvious artifices. It is
enough to compare his prose with that of Nicholas of
Clairvaux, his contemporary who was for a time his 'notary',
to appreciate the refinement of the means Bernard employed.
These flashes of insight must have taxed him little: with a
quickness commensurate to a task which occupied his spare

time, and without doubt amused him, he perfected his text by means of corrections similar to those which one makes in haste on proofsheets. It is because he was an excellent writer that he was never satisfied with himself. These demands of a literary character were in him a reflection of a deeper preoccupation: the pursuit of a perfection not only aesthetic but also moral. The business of correcting a text already composed has always been designated, in the Latin tradition, as *emendatio*. Now this same word was always translated, in ascetic language, as the correction of vices, of faults, of imperfections. An antiphon sung at the beginning of Lent, the time of penitence, began with the words *Emendemus in melius . . . ,* 'Let us improve ourselves for the better . . . '. In applying to himself and to his texts this effort which he never ceased to ask of his monks, he succeeded in making the *Sermons on the Song of Songs* a masterpiece whose splendor numberless readers have perceived. The beauty of the book explains its influence.

One could sometimes be tempted to regret that Bernard of Clairvaux wrote nothing in his own hand and left no autographs one could preserve, as was the case with Teresa of Avila and Thérèse of Lisieux. Yet a knowledge of the working methods of the twelfth century excluded such hypotheses. There does exist a study bearing on the 'handwriting of the saints',[14] but the first text with which the author could deal dates back to nearly a century after St Bernard. Even then it is only a short document coming from the pen of St Francis. Later in the course of the thirteenth century, there are some examples of lengthy texts written by the hand of St Bonaventure and St Thomas. They remain exceptionally rare, however, even from these two great authors. The major part of their work was 'dictated' in conditions very like those of the time of St Bernard.[15]

Happily the literary quality of the *Sermons on the Song of Songs* has assured their success, and consequently occasioned the reproduction of manuscripts sufficiently numerous to allow us not only to reconstitute Bernard's work, but to be witnesses to the way in which he produced it. On the other hand, even the homelier sermons that were delivered verbally but not 'dictated' by Bernard possessed enough charm to be put in writing and then reproduced in numerous copies. The styles proper to each of these two categories of works are diverse. Both authentic, they cause one another to be appreciated. In both cases, Bernard at one and the same time transmits a doctrinal message and clothes it with this human quality that helps the word of God to enter deep into the heart.

Jean Leclercq

Translated by Kathleen Waters OCSO

NOTES

1.   On the meaning of these different terms, I have given some information (examples, references, bibliography) in *Recueil d'études sur S. Bernard*, I, (Rome, 1962) p. 3–25; in *Etudes sur S. Bernard et le texte de ses écrits*, (Rome, *Analecta SOC;* IX, 1–2, 1953). Others will be found in a study in preparation in *Dictare*. Already there is some information in 'Pour l'histoire du canif et de la lime,' in *Scriptorium* 26 (1972), 294–300.

2.   See, for example, the remarkable thesis of Malachy Marion, *Petitionary Prayer in Mark and in the* Q *Material,* Ann Arbor, University Microfilms, no. 74–20.162.

3.   *Recueil d'études*, I:213–274; *Introduction à S. Bernardi opera*, I; *Sermones super Cantica canticorum* (Rome, 1957).

4.   These problems have been studied by A.H. Bredero, 'Etudes sur la "Vita prima" de S. Bernard', in *Analecta SOC* 17 (1961) 3–72, 215–260; 18 (1962) 3–59.

5.   Concerning the examples that have just been cited, bibliography in *Recueil d'études*, I:269, n.269.

6.   *Recueil*, I:175–190; 'Poéme inspiré de S. Bernard', in *Analecta SOC*, 7 (1951) 58–60.

7.   In *Monks and Love in Twelfth Century France* (Oxford, 1979) 8–26, 86–108, I have given bibliographic and other information.

8.   Bernard, *De consideratione*, I.12; *S. Bernardi opera*, IV (Rome, 1963) 407–408.

9.   *De consideratione*, II.1–4; *SBOP*, IV:410–413.

10.   Eph 5:8, cited at the end of Sermon 86:4.

11.   Under the title 'Essais sur l'esthétique de S. Bernard', in *Studi medievali*, 9 (1968) 688–728, I have described this doctrine and this practice.

12.   These statements are illustrated by examples in *Recueil*, I: 298–319.

13.   References are given in *Recueil*, I:232, 333, 351, n. 4.

14.   G. Moretti, *I santi dalla loro scrittura. Esami grafologici* (Rome, 1975).

15.   Cf. H. Dondaine, *Secrétaires de S. Thomas* (Rome, 1956).

BERNARD OF CLAIRVAUX

ON THE SONG OF SONGS, IV

1

SERMON SIXTY-SEVEN

I. TO WHOM THE BRIDE SPEAKS WHEN
SHE SAYS 'MY BELOVED IS MINE' ETC.,
AND HOW THE BRIDEGROOM'S REPLY IS
LIKE A BANQUET. II. THAT IT IS BET-
TER TO SUPPOSE SHE IS SPEAKING TO
HERSELF; AND THE REASON FOR THIS
INCOMPLETE CONVERSATION. III. HOW
THE WORD OF THE BRIDE IS AN UTTER-
ANCE, SWEET TO THE TASTE AND FRA-
GRANT; THE JUST MAN TASTES IT, AND
THE SINNER CATCHES ITS FRAGRANCE.
IV. OF THE ACCEPTANCE OF THE EX-
PECTATION WHICH THE JUST EXPECTS,
WHILE THE SINNER HAS NOTHING TO
HOPE FOR; AND OF THE UTTERANCE OF
DAVID, AND OF THE APOSTLES JOHN
AND PAUL. V. WHAT IS TO BE INFERRED
FROM THESE WORDS, AND THE ORDER
OF WORDS USED BY THE BRIDE AND THE
PROPHET. VI. OF PREVENIENT AND
SUBSEQUENT GRACE.

Sg 2:16

'**M**Y BELOVED is mine and I am
his.'* It is the bridegroom
I. 1   whose words we have pondered
until now. We implore his presence that we
may worthily trace the words of his Bride, to
his glory and for our salvation, for we cannot
worthily consider and study such words as
these unless he is present to guide our discourse.* For her words are pleasant and lovely,
bringing profit to the understanding, and
they are deep in mystery. To what shall I compare them? They are like a banquet which
excels all others, threefold, delicious to the
taste, giving true nourishment, and rich in
healing power. So is every word of the Bride;
and while it is sweet to hear, it delights the
affections and enriches the mind, nourishing
it with its wealth of meaning and its deep
mysteries. The spirit is filled with dread even
while it is stirred; the canker of pride swollen
by learning is miraculously healed.* But if
anyone who imagines that he has a smattering
of knowledge indulges in too close an inquiry,
he will find his intellectual powers overcome
and his whole mind reduced to subjection.*
How humbled he will be at her words, con-
strained to say: 'Such knowledge is too
wonderful for me; it is mighty and I cannot
attain to it.'* What sweetness marks her
opening words!† See how she begins her
song: 'My beloved is mine and I am his!'* Her
words seem simple, and their sound is sweet.
We shall consider this after a while.

2. She begins with love, and goes on to
speak of the beloved, declaring that she knows
no other than the beloved.* Of whom she

Ac 14:11

1 Cor 8:1

2 Cor 10:5

Ps 138:5 (Vulgate
enumeration)
†Ps 118:160
*Sg 2:16

1 Cor 2:2

speaks is clear, but not to whom. We cannot suppose that she is speaking to the Bridegroom, since he is not present. That is not in question, for she appears to be calling him back to her, crying 'Return, my beloved.'*   *Sg 2:17* Hence we cannot but believe that when he had ended his words he withdrew again, according to his custom, yet she continued to speak of him who was never absent from her. Thus it was; he was still on her lips and had not left her heart nor ever would. The words which came from her mouth came from her heart, and it was from the fulness of her heart that she spoke.* Therefore it is of the   *Lk 6:45,* beloved she speaks, she who is herself beloved   *Mt 15:18* and truly to be loved, since she loved much.*   *Lk 7:47* We ask to whom she speaks, for we know of whom. There is no answer, unless perhaps she speaks with her handmaidens, who cannot leave their mistress while the Bridegroom is away.

II. I think it better to suppose she is speaking to herself, not to another, especially as her words appear abrupt and disconnected, insufficient to communicate knowledge to the hearer, which is the chief object of conversation. 'My beloved is mine and I am his.' Nothing more? The words hover—no, they do not hover, they fall. The hearer is left in suspense; he receives no communication, but his interest is aroused.

3. What is this that she says: 'He is mine and I am his'? We do not know what she says, because we do not know what she feels.*   *Jn 16:18* O holy soul, what is your beloved to you?

What are you to him? What is this intimate
relationship, this pledge given and received?
He is yours, you in turn are his. But are you
to him what he is to you, or is there some
difference? If you will, speak to us, to our
understanding, tell us clearly what you feel.*
How long will you keep us in expectation? Is
your secret to be for you alone?* It is thus:
it is the *affectus,* not the intellect, which has
spoken, and it is not for the intellect to grasp.
What then is the reason for these words? There
is none, except that the Bride is transported
with delight and enraptured by the long-
awaited words of the Bridegroom, and when
words ceased she could neither keep silence
nor yet express what she felt. Nor did she
speak thus to express her feelings but merely
to break her silence. 'Out of the fulness of the
heart the mouth speaks,'* but not in the same
measure. The *affectus* have their own language,
in which they disclose themselves even against
their will. Fear has its trembling, grief its
anguished groans, love its cries of delight. Are
the lamentations of mourners, the sobs of
those who grieve, the sighs of those in pain,
the sudden frenzied screams of those in fear,
the yawns of the replete—are these the result
of habit? Do they constitute a reasoned discourse, a deliberate utterance, a premeditated
speech? Most certainly such expressions of
feeling are not produced by the processes
of the mind, but by spontaneous impulses. So
a strong and burning love, particularly the
love of God, does not stop to consider the
order, the grammar, the flow, or the number
of the words it employs, when it cannot

Jn 10:24

Is 24:16

Lk 6:45

contain itself, providing it senses that it suffers no loss thereby. Sometimes it needs no words, no expression at all, being content with aspirations alone. Thus it is that the Bride, aflame with holy love, doubtless seeking to quench a little the fire of the love she endures, gives no thought to her words or the manner of her speech, but impelled by love she does not speak clearly, but bursts out with whatever comes into her mouth. How should she not do so when she is thus refreshed and satisfied?

4. Turn again to the words of this marriage-song from its beginning to this point, and see whether in all their trysts and colloquies such tenderness has ever been shown to the Bride, and whether she has ever heard so many delightful words from his mouth. When she has satisfied her desires with good things,* why should it be strange if she utters a cry rather than words; or, if she seems to form words, that they should be inarticulate, not polished or well-chosen. The Bride thinks it no robbery* to take to herself the words of the Prophet: 'My heart has belched a goodly theme,'* since she is filled with the same spirit.

III. 'My beloved is mine, and I am his'.* There is no conclusion here, no prayer. What is there? It is a belch. Why should you look to find connected prayers or solemn declarations in a belch? What rules or regulations do you impose upon yours? They do not admit of your control, or wait for you to compose them, nor do they consult your

Ps 102:5

Ph 2:6

Ps 44:2

Sg 2:16

leisure or convenience. They burst forth from
within, without your will or knowledge, torn
from you rather than uttered. But a belch
gives out an odor, sometimes good, sometimes
bad, according to the quality of the vessel
they come from. Now a good man out of his
good treasure brings forth good things, and an
Mt 12:35 evil man evil things!* The Bride of my Lord is
a vessel of good things, and the odor which
comes from her is sweet.

5. I thank you, Lord Jesus, who have
deigned to allow me at least to sense that
odor. Yes, Lord, for the dogs eat the crumbs
Mt 15:27 which come from the rich man's table.* The
breath of your beloved is to me a goodly odor,
Jn 1:16 and I receive of its fulness gratefully,* in however small measure. For it causes the memory
Ps 144:7 of your abundant sweetness to arise in me,*
and I find the ineffable sweetness of your
condescending love in this saying: 'My beloved
is mine and I am his.' Let her feast and
Ps 67:4 rejoice in your sight, and delight in your joy.*
Let her be beside herself for you that she may
be sober for us. Let her be filled with the good
2 Cor 5:13 things of your house,* and drink of the river
Ps 35:9 of your pleasure.* But, I beg, let but a light
fragrance from her abundance come to me, a
poor man. Moses belched for my profit and
there is a goodly fragrance from his belching
about the power of creation. 'In the beginning', he said, 'God created heaven and
Gen 1:1 earth.* Isaiah uttered profitable words for
me, for he gave forth the sweet fragrance of
mercy and redemption, when he belched: 'He
Is 53:12 has poured out his soul unto death;* he was
numbered with the transgressors; he himself

bore the sins of many and made intercession
for the transgressors,* that they shall not   *Is 38:17*
perish.' What smells of mercy like that? Good
also is the word which comes from the mouth
of Jeremiah, and good that which came from
David, who said 'My heart has belched a
goodly theme.'* They were all filled with the   *Ps 44:2*
Holy Ghost,* and their belchings filled all   *Ac 2:3*
things with goodness.* Do you ask for Jere-   *Ps 103:28*
miah's belch? I have not forgotten; I was
building up to it. 'It is good that a man should
wait in silence for the salvation of God.* It is   *Lam 3:26*
his, I am not making a mistake. Breathe it in;
the sweetness it exudes is that of one who
rewards justice, sweeter than balsam. He
chooses that I should suffer for righteousness'
sake and wait for my reward hereafter. I shall
not receive it now, because the reward of
justice is salvation,* not as the world knows   *Wis 2:2*
it, but the salvation of God. 'Though the
vision tarry, wait for it,'* he says, and adds,   *Hab 2:3*
so that you will not murmur, 'it is good to
wait in silence.'* Therefore I shall do what he   *Lam 3:26*
commands; I shall wait for the Lord my
Saviour.*   *Mic 7:7*
    6. But I am a sinner,* and a long road   *Lk 5:8*
still awaits me;* for salvation is far from the   *1 Kg 19:7*
wicked.* Yet I will not murmur; until then I   *Ps 118:155*
shall console myself with its fragrance. The
righteous shall rejoice in the Lord,* tasting   *Ps 63:11*
and knowing what I only perceive by its
fragrance. He whom the righteous sees face to
face, the sinner awaits; and the waiting is
fragrance. 'For the earnest expectation of the
creature waits for the revelation of the sons
of God.* And to see is to taste, and to know   *Rom 8:19*

Ps 33:9   how gracious the Lord is.*

IV. Perhaps it is instead the righteous man
who awaits it, and the blessed who possesses
Prov 10:28   it. The hope of the righteous is joy,* but a
sinner has nothing to hope for. Therefore,
because the sinner is not only attached to the
good things of this present world, but is also
satisfied with them, he does not set his hope
on the future and is deaf to this call. 'Wait',
said the Lord, 'wait for the day of my rising
Zeph 3:8   that is to come.'* Simeon was righteous because he waited in hope and already knew the
fragrance of Christ in his spirit, though he did
not yet adore him in the flesh; and blessed was
he in his expectation, and through the fragrance of his expectation, and through the
fragrance of expectation he came to the taste
of contemplation. Then he said: 'Mine eyes
Lk 2:25   have seen thy salvation.'* Abraham was right-
Lk 2:30   eous, waiting to see the day of the Lord,*
Ps 118:116   and he was not disappointed of his hope,*
Jn 8:56   for he saw it and rejoiced.* The Apostles
were righteous, to whom it was said, 'You
yourselves are like men who wait for their
Lk 12:36   Lord.'*

7. Was David not righteous when he said
Ps 39:2   'I waited patiently for the Lord'?* He is the
fourth of those whose utterances I have men-
tioned. I had almost passed him by. But that
2 Cor 12:1   would not be right. He opened his mouth†
†Ps 118:131   and drew in his breath, and when he was
filled full he not only belched but also sang.
Good Jesus! With what sweetness he suffused
my nostrils and my ears when he belched and
sang of the oil of gladness with which God

anointed him above his fellows,* and of   *Ps 44:8*
'myrrh and aloes and cassia from your vest-
ments, from the ivory palaces, with which the
king's daughters have honored you and made
you glad'.* If only you would count me   *Ps 44:9-10*
worthy of meeting such a prophet, such a
friend of yours in the day of solemn gladness,
when he comes forth from your chamber,*   *Jl 2:16*
singing his marriage-song in joyful psalmody
with the harp,* shedding abroad his de-   *Ps 80:3*
lights, scattering and strewing everywhere
every powdery pigment.* In that day, in   *Sg 3:6*
that hour—if there is an hour then, and it may
be not even an hour, but half an hour, according to the words of Scripture: 'There was
silence in heaven for about the space of
half-an-hour'*—in that hour my mouth shall   *Rev 8:1*
be filled with joy and my tongue with glad-
ness,* for I shall sense the fragrance of every   *Ps 125:2*
Psalm, not merely of every Psalm, but of
every Psalm, every verse, every belch, more
fragrant than any perfume.* What is more   *Sg 2:10*
fragrant than the belch of John, who makes
sweet for me the eternal generation and
divinity of the Word? What shall I say about
Paul's belches, how they have filled the world
with sweetness? Now the sweet savor of
Christ is everywhere.* Although he does not   *2 Cor 2:15*
allow me to hear the ineffable words, yet
truly he bids me desire them, and I may
freely catch the fragrance of what I may not
hear.* For some unknown reason, what is   *2 Cor 12:4*
hidden is most desirable, and we long most
strongly for what is denied us.

V. But now notice how it is the same with

the Bride: how, like Paul in the passage we are considering, she does not reveal her secret, nor yet leave it without mention, for she is pleased to give us some satisfaction, allowed us to catch the fragrance of the mystery which through our unworthiness or weakness she sees we are not fit to taste.

Sg 2:16
8. 'My beloved is mine, and I am his.'* There is no doubt that in this passage a shared love blazes up, but a love in which one of them experiences the highest felicity, while the other shows marvellous condescension. This is no betrothal or union of equals here. Who could lay claim to any clear knowledge of the nature of this token of love in which she glories, bestowed upon her and repaid again by her? Who indeed, except one worthy himself of a like experience, being pure in soul and holy in body? Its reality is in the affections; it is not to be attained by reason but by affections by conformity. How few there are who can say: 'But we all, with unveiled face, beholding the glory of the Lord, are being changed into his likeness from glory into glory, even by the Spirit of the Lord.'*

2 Cor 3:18
9. Now let us put these words into some from which can be grasped by the intellect. The Bride's own secret must be preserved, for we may not yet attain to it, being what we are. Let us therefore consider something better suited to our common sense and of a more familiar nature, something which derives from her words and gives understanding to the simple.* I think it should satisfy our blunted and untutored understanding if we take the words 'My beloved is mine' to mean,

Ps 118:130

'inclines', so the meaning is: 'My beloved inclines to me, and I to him.' I am not the only one to suggest this meaning, nor the first, for the Prophet before me said: 'I waited patiently for the Lord and he inclined to me.'* *Ps 39:2* You note clearly the way in which the Lord inclines to the Prophet, and the Prophet to the Lord, when he says, 'I waited patiently', for he who waits inclines towards the one for whom he waits, and to wait for anyone is to incline towards him. Thus the meaning of the words, and even the words themselves, are the same as those of the Bride, but their order is reversed, so that what he puts first she puts last, and vice versa.

10. But it is the Bride who speaks more directly, for she does not pretend to any merit, but mentions first the kindness she has received, acknowledging that the grace of the Beloved goes before her. She does well. For 'who has first given a gift to him, and been recompensed by him?'* Now hear John's *Rom 11:35* reflections on this: 'In this is love', he says, 'not that we loved God, but that he first loved us.'* And even though the Prophet is silent *1 Jn 4:10* about the grace that precedes, he does beyond all doubt speak about that which follows. Now listen in another passage to an even clearer statement on this subject: 'Your mercy will follow me all the days of my life.'* And *Ps 22:6* there is an equally emphatic statement about prevenient [grace]: 'My God, his mercy shall go before me',* and again to the Lord [he *Ps 58:11* says]: 'Let your mercies speedily go before us, for we have been brought very low.'* *Ps 78:8*

VI. A little later the Bride uses the same words again, unless I am mistaken, but not in the same order. With exquisite subtlety, she follows the order of the Prophet and says: 'I am my Beloved's and he is mine.'* Why this? Surely that she may show herself more full of grace* when she surrenders wholly to grace, attributing to him both the beginning and the ending. How indeed could she be full of grace if there were any part of her which did not itself spring from grace? There is no way for grace to enter, if [a sense of] merit has taken residence in the soul. A full acknowledgement of grace then is a sign of the fulness of grace. Indeed if the soul possesses anything of its own, to that extent grace must give place to it; whatever you impute to merit you steal from grace. I want nothing to do with the sort of merit which excludes grace. I shrink from whatever I possess, that I may truly possess myself, unless that which makes me my own is to some extent my own. Grace restores me to myself, freely justified,* and thus sets me free from the bondage of sin. For where the Spirit is, there is liberty.*

11. See that foolish bride, the Synagogue, who took no account of the justice of God,* that is the grace of the Bridegroom, but chose to set up her own, owing no allegiance to the justice of God.* Therefore the unhappy bride was put away, and it is no longer she who is the Bride, but the Church, to whom is said: 'I have betrothed you to myself in faith, in judgment and justice, in mercy and pity.* For you have not chosen me but I have chosen you;*

Sg 6:2

Lk 1:28

Rom 8:21

2 Cor 3:17

Wis 14:30

Rom 10:3

Hos 2:19
Jn 15:16

not for any merits that I found in you did I choose you, but I went before you. Thus have I betrothed you to myself in faith, not in the works of the law;* in justice indeed, but the justice which is of faith, not of the law.* Now you may give right judgment between us,* the judgment in which I betrothed you to myself, whereby it is established that it is not your merits which mediate between us, but my pleasure. This is the judgment,* that you do not extol your merits or uphold the works of the law, or bear the burden and heat of the day,* but rather be known as betrothed in faith, in the justice which is of faith,* in mercy and pity.'*

Rom 3:20

Rom 9:30

Ps 118:154

Jn 3:19

Mt 20:12

Rom 9:30

Ps 102:4

12. She who is the true Bride acknowledges this, and recognizes each grace—first that which is first because it goes before, then that which follows. Therefore she says first: 'My beloved is mine and I am his',* ascribing to the Beloved the beginning; then she follows with: 'I am my beloved's and he is mine,'* conceding to him equally the end. Now let us observe that she says 'My beloved is mine'. If we may supply, as I suggested before, 'inclines himself to me'—as the Prophet says, 'I waited patiently for the Lord and he inclined unto me'.* I find in that word something far from insignificant, something of considerable importance. But you are tired of listening. I must not inflict on you a subject which needs all your attention. If it does not incommode you, I will defer it, but only for a little. Tomorrow I will begin with it. Only pray that we may be preserved meanwhile from all disturbance by the mercy of the Bride-

Sg 2:16

Sg 6:2

Ps 39:2

Wis 14:15
Rom 9:5

groom of the Church,* Jesus Christ our Lord,
who is God above all, blessed for ever.*
Amen.

SERMON SIXTY-EIGHT

I. OF THE CARE OF THE BRIDEGROOM
FOR THE BRIDE, AND HER CARE FOR
HIM: HOW SHE IS HIS ONLY CARE.
II. HOW THE END OF ALL THINGS DE-
PENDS ON THE STATE AND CONSUMMA-
TION OF THE CHURCH. III. OF THE
MERITS AND CONFIDENCE OF THE
CHURCH, AND THE SOURCE OF HER
MERITS.

I. 1. **H**EAR NOW what I held over from yesterday; hear of the joy which I have experienced. Yet it is your joy also. Hear of it then and rejoice. I experienced this joy in just one word of the Bride; and I was, as it were, lapped in its fragrance; so I hid it away to bring out for you today, all the more joyfully because it is more opportune. The Bride has spoken, and has said that the Bridegroom inclines himself to her;* who then is the Bride, and who is the Bridegroom? The Bridegroom is our God,* and we, I say in all humility, are the Bride— we, and the whole multitude of captives whom he acknowledges. Let us rejoice that this glory is ours;* we are they to whom God inclines. But how unequal a partnership! What are the earth-born, the children of

Sg 5:6
Ps 47:15

2 Cor 1:12

17

Ps 48:3

men,* in his presence? In the words of the Prophet Isaiah, 'they are as if they were not, they are considered by him as nothing but emptiness.'* What meaning can there be in a comparison between such different persons? Either the Bride glorifies herself beyond measure, or the Bridegroom loves beyond measure. How wonderful that she should claim as her own the attention of the Bridegroom when she says, 'My beloved is mine'.* Nor is she yet content, but goes on to glorify herself even more, replying to him in her turn as to an equal; for she continues, 'and I am his'. A wonderful saying—'and I am his'; and no less wonderful, 'My Beloved is mine'. But that both should be said together—that is more wonderful than either.

Is 40:17

Sg 2:16

2. There is nothing that a pure heart, a good conscience, and an unfeigned faith will not venture.* 'He inclines to me', says the Bride. Does this great majesty incline to her thus—this majesty on whom rests the government and administration of the universe? Does the care of the world give way to the business—or rather the repose—of the love and desire of the Bride? Yes indeed, for she is the Church of the elect, of whom the Apostle Paul says, 'I endure everything for the sake of the elect'.* And who can doubt that God shows grace and mercy to his saints,* and is mindful of his elect. Therefore we cannot deny his providence towards the rest of his creatures; but the Bride claims his attention for herself. Is it for oxen that God is concerned?* No doubt we can say the same about horses, camels, elephants, and all the

1 Tim 1:5

2 Tim 2:10
Wis 4:15

1 Cor 9:9

beasts on earth and the fishes in the sea and
the birds of the air;* indeed of everything on   *Gen 1:26*
the earth except only those to whom is said,
'Casting all your care upon him for he cares
for you.'* Do you not see that this is the same   *1 Pet 5:7*
as saying, 'Incline to him, for he inclines to
you'? And notice that the Apostle Peter,
whose words these are, preserves the same
order of words as does the Bride, for he says,
'Casting all your care upon him'*—not 'in   *Ibid.*
order that he may care for you' but 'because
he cares for you,'* thereby revealing not only   *Ps 88:6*
the depth of his love for the Church of the
Saints,* but also its eternal quality.   *Ps 149:1*

3. It is obvious that what the Apostle says
about oxen* has no reference to the Bride; he   *1 Cor 9:9*
who loves her and gave himself for her* must   *Gal 1:4*
needs care for her.* Is she not that lost   *Lk 10:35*
sheep* whose care came before even that of   *Mt 18:12*
the heavenly flock?* The shepherd left the   *1 Pet 2:25*
rest and came to earth to find her. He sought
her diligently, and when he found her* he did   *Lk 15:5*
not lead her, but carried her back! Then on
her account he called the angels together and
celebrated a new and joyful festival with her.
How then can it be said that he will not care
for her,* when he deigned to carry her on his   *Lk 10:35*
shoulders? She is not mistaken,* then, when   *Heb 2:11*
she says, 'The Lord takes thought for me',*   *Ps 39:18*
nor is she deceived when she says, 'The Lord
will fulfil his purpose for me'*, or when she   *Ps 137:8*
says anything else which shows God's love for
her. Thus it is that she speaks of the Lord
of Hosts as her beloved, and glories* that he   *Wis 12:18*
who judges all things in tranquillity* cares for   *1 Cor 2:15*
her. Why should she not glory? She has heard

him saying to her, 'Can a woman forget her child, and not have compassion on him? And even if she does forget him, yet I will not forget you.'* Again, 'The eyes of the Lord are upon the righteous.'* Now what is the Bride but the congregation of the righteous? What is she but the generation of those who seek the face of the Bridegroom?* It cannot be that he should incline to her, and she not incline to him. Therefore she says, 'He inclines to me and I to him. He inclines to me because he is good and gracious;* I incline to him because I am not ungrateful. He gives me grace from his graciousness;* I give him gratitude for grace. He has a care for my deliverance and my salvation; I for his honor and the fulfilment of his will. He has a care for me, and for no other, for I am his only dove;* I have a care for him and for no other;* I do not hear the voice of others, nor do I listen to those who say "Look, here is Christ" or "look, there he is!" '* It is the Church who speaks.

II. 4.   What shall we say, each one of us? Do we think that there is any among us to whom the Bride's words can be applied? Do I say 'Any among us'? I think myself that any inquiry would show that there is no member of the Church to whom it may not be applied in some degree. But one does not deal with an individual in the same way as with many people. It was not for one soul, but for many who should be gathered up into the one Church, his only Bride, that God wrought so great a work at so great a cost, 'working salvation in the midst of the earth'.* She is the

Margin references:
Is 49:15
Ps 33:16

Ps 23:6

Jl 2:13

Jn 1:16

Sg 6:8
Jn 10:15

Mk 13:21

Ps 73:12

only one, the dearest of all to him, embracing him as no other spouse, as he gives himself to no other Bride. What may she not ask from so generous a love? What may she not hope for from one who came from heaven to seek her,* who called her to him from the ends of the earth, and bought her at a price—the price of the blood of him who bought her. Moreover, her confidence is the greater when she looks to the future and knows that the Lord has need of her.* Do you ask why? To see the prosperity of his chosen ones,* to rejoice in the gladness of his people, to glory with his heritage. You must not think that this is a small matter. I tell you that none of his works will reach perfection if this one fails. Does not the end of all things depend on the condition and consummation of the Church? Take away this, and the lower creation will wait in vain for the revelation of the sons of God.* Take away this, then neither patriarchs nor prophets will come to perfection, for Paul says that God has ordained for us that apart from us they should not be made perfect.* Take away this, and the very glory of the holy angels will be impaired if their numbers are not complete, nor will the City of God rejoice in its wholeness.

5. How then shall the design of God find fulfillment,* that mystery of his will† and sacrament of his mercy?* How shall I be given those babes and sucklings out of whose mouth God has perfected praise?* It is not heaven, but the Church, where these children are found, to whom is said, 'I feed you with milk, not solid food'.* And they are invited to

Acts 20:28

Mt 21:3
Ps 105:5

Rom 8:19

Heb 11:40

*Rom 9:11
†Eph 1:9
*1 Tim 3:16

Ps 8:3

1 Cor 3:2

complete, as it were, the glory of God, in
the words of the prophet, 'Praise the Lord,
you children'.* Do you imagine that God will
receive all the praise due his glory before the
the coming of those who shall sing in the
presence of the angels,* 'We rejoice for the
days in which you have humiliated us, for
the years in which we have seen evil'?* Even
the heavens do not know this kind of joy,
except through the children of the Church;
no-one experiences joy like this unless he has
known what it is to be without joy. Joy is
most welcome after sadness, rest after toil,
harbor after shipwreck. Everyone enjoys se-
curity, but no-one so much as one who has
known fear. Light is pleasant to everyone, but
particularly to someone who has escaped
from the tyranny of darkness.* To have passed
from death to life doubles the beauty of life.*
This is my offering to the common life of
heaven, and it is something of which the
blessed spirits have no knowledge. I would
even dare to say that the very life of the
blessed lacks that blessedness which is mine,
unless they acknowledge that they enjoy it
through charity in me and through me. Something of my own bliss seems to be added even
to that perfection, and this is no small matter, for the angels rejoice at a sinner's repen-
tance.* And if my tears are a joy to the angels,
what must my joy be? All they do is in praise
of God; but something is lacking in that praise
if there is none to say 'We passed through fire
and water, and you led us to a place of
refreshment'.*

Ps 112:1

Ps 137:1

Ps 89:15

Col 1:13

Jn 5:24

Lk 15:10

Ps 65:12

III. 6. Happy then is the Church in her completeness, yet all her praise is unequal to him
who occasions it, not only for the blessings
she has received, but also for those yet to be
given her.* Why should she be anxious about   *Rev 1:1*
her merits, when she has a stronger, surer
reason for exultation in the purpose of God?*   *Rom 9:11*
God cannot contradict himself, nor cause
not to be done what he has done, for, as the
Scripture says, 'He has done what is to be'.*   *Qo 3:15*
He will do so, he will do so; he will not fail in
his purpose. Therefore you have no need to
ask on what merits we base our hope, especially when you hear the word of the prophet
Ezekiel:* 'It is not for your sake that I do   *Ez 36:22*
this, but for my own,' says the Lord. It is
enough for merit to know that merit is not
enough. But as merit must not presume on
merit, so lack of merit must bring judgment.
Furthermore, children re-born in baptism
are not without merit, but possess the merits
of Christ; but they make themselves unworthy
of these if they do not add their own—not
because of inability, but because of neglect;
this is the danger of maturity. Henceforward,
take care that you possess merit; when you
possess it, you will know it as a gift. Hope for
its fruit, the mercy of God, and you will
escape all danger of poverty, ingratitude, and
presumption. The lack of merit is a poverty
which destroys, but presumption of spirit is
false riches.* Therefore the wise man says,   *Qo 6:9*
'Give me neither poverty nor riches'.* Happy   *Cf. Prov 30:8*
is the Church which does not lack merits free
from presumption nor presumption free from
merits. She has grounds for presumption, but

they are not her merits. Merits she has, but they
are to be earned, not presumed upon. Not to
presume upon anything: is this not to have a
claim upon it? So she is more secure in presum-
ing upon that which she does not presume upon, and she has no cause to find difficulty in the
expression of her exultation,* since she has
much ground for exaltation.* The mercies of
God are many,* and his truth endures forever.†

7. Why should she not exult in safety,
since mercy and truth are met together* as a
proof of her glory? Therefore whether she
says 'My beloved is mine',* or 'I waited for
the Lord and he inclined to me',* or even
'The Lord takes thought of me'* or uses some
other such words which seem to express God's
love and singular favor towards one of his
creatures, she will find none of these things
foreign to her, since the ground of her confidence is the nature of God. Then, too, she sees
no other Bride, no other Church, in whom can
be fulfilled what must be fulfilled. Therefore,
as far as the Church is concerned, it is clear
that she will in no way hesitate to claim all
these promises for herself. You may ask
whether it is permissible for any one soul,
however spiritual and holy, to venture to act
thus; for surely all the favors ordained for the
great body catholic may not be claimed for
herself by one soul, of whatever degree of
sanctity, out of all that great number. So I
feel it may be somewhat difficult, if indeed it
is possible, to find how this may be permitted.
Therefore I think this must be dealt with in
another sermon, and we must not now enter
the toils of so intricate a subject, whose

Si 47:9

Si 47:9
*Ps 118:156
†Ps 116:2

Ps 84:11

Sg 2:16

Ps 39:2

Ps 39:18

outcome we do not yet know, without first
making our prayer on this profound matter*   *Job 4:12*
to him who opens and no-one closes,* the   *Rev 3:7*
Bridegroom of the Church, Jesus Christ our
Lord, who is God above all, blessed for ever.*   *Rom 9:5*
Amen.

SERMON SIXTY-NINE

I. WHAT SOUL MAY RIGHTLY SAY 'MY
BELOVED IS MINE' ETC., AND WITH WHAT
JUSTIFICATION. II. OF THE COMING
OF THE FATHER AND THE SON TO THE
SOUL, AND HOW THE WRATH AND ANGER
OF THE FATHER OVERTHROWS ALL PRE-
SUMPTION IN THE SOUL. III. OF THE
BURNING CHARITY IN WHICH THE
FATHER AND SON COME, AND OF THEIR
INDWELLING; AND BY WHAT MEANS THE
SOUL BECOMES AWARE OF IT.

Sg 2:16

1 Tim 4:8

Dan 7:20
Ps 39:2

I. 1. '**M**Y BELOVED is mine, and I am his.'* In my last sermon I attributed this saying to the Church Universal, because of the promises made to her by God* in this present life as well as in the life to come. The question was raised whether it was possible for an individual soul to claim for itself what the whole Church might claim without presumption, or whether indeed it could appropriate the promise to itself in any way at all. If this may not be done, we must apply it to the church in such a way that it may not refer to any individual— and not only this saying, but others like it which express great truths,* like 'I waited for the Lord and he inclined to me'*, and others

26

which were mentioned in the last sermon. If
you think that they apply to the individual,
I would not contradict you. But this is a
matter of some importance, for it cannot apply to everyone indiscriminately. Certainly
there are within the Church of God spiritual
persons who serve him faithfully and with
confidence,* speaking with him as a man   *Jn 14:23*
speaks with his friend,* and whose con-   *Ex 33:11*
sciences bear witness to his glory.* But who   *Rom 9:1*
these are is known only to God,* and if you   *Ph 1:21*
desire to be among them, then hear what sort
of people you should be. I say this, not as
one who knows it by experience, but as one
who desires to do so. Show me a soul which
loves nothing but God and what is to be
loved for God's sake, to whom to live is
Christ,* and of whom this has been true   *Ps 15:8*
for a long time now; who in work and leisure
alike endeavors to keep God before his eyes,
and walks humbly with the Lord his God;*   *Mi 6:8*
who desires that his will may be one with the
will of God, and who has been given the grace
to do these things. Show me a soul like this,
and I will not deny that she is worthy of the
Bridegroom's care, of the regard of God's
majesty, of his sovereign favor, and of the
attention of his goverance. And if she is
minded to boast, she will not be a fool,* so *2 Cor 12:6*
long as she who boasts boasts in the Lord.*   *1 Cor 1:31*
Thus what many dare to boast of,* one may   *2 Cor 11:21*
also dare, though for a different reason.

2. These considerations do indeed give
confidence to the many faithful, but there are
two which apply to the faithful soul. First,
the essential simplicity of the Godhead is able

to see many persons as if they were one, and one as if he were many, without division of attention between many or restriction to one, with no diminishment on the one hand or intensification on the other, being neither disturbed by anxieties nor troubled by cares; thus he may occupy himself with one without preoccupation, and with many without distraction. Next, a thing very sweet to experience, as it is very rare; such is the courtesy of the Word, such the tenderness of the Father towards the well-disposed, well-ordered soul— itself the gift of the Father and the work of the Son—that they honor with their own presence the one whom they have foreordained and prepared for themselves, and not only do they come to him, but they make their dwelling-place with him.* For it is not enough that their presence is revealed; they must also give of their fulness.

1 Cor 8:1

II. What does it mean for the Word to come into a soul? It means that he will instruct it in wisdom.* What does it mean for the Father to come? It means that he will draw it to the love of wisdom, so that it may say, 'I was a lover of her beauty'.* It is the Father's nature to love, and therefore the coming of the Father is marked by an infusion of love. What would happen to learning apart from love? It would be puffed up.* What would happen to love apart from learning? It would go astray, as they went astray of whom it was said, 'I grant that they have a zeal for God but it is not according to knowledge'.* It is not fitting that the Bride of the Word should be ignorant;

Ps 89:12

Ws 8:2

1 Cor 8:1

Rom 10:2

moreover the Bridegroom does not allow the Bride to be uplifted with pride; for the Father loves the Son* and never hesitates to cast down and to destroy* whatever sets itself up against the knowledge of the Word, tempering zeal through judgment or increasing it through mercy. May he cast down in me all pride: destroy it, reduce it to nothingness, not by his blazing anger but by his welling love. May I learn not to be proud, but by the tutelage of anointing rather than of avenging. Lord, rebuke me not in your indignation,* as you did the angel who exalted himself, neither chasten me in your wrath,* as you did man in paradise. Both were resolved on wickedness,* aspiring to exalt themselves, the one through power, the other through knowledge. For the woman foolishly believed the deceiver's promise: 'You shall be gods, when you know good and evil'.* He had already deceived himself; when he persuaded himself that he would be like the Most High.* For he who thinks himself to be something when he is nothing deceives himself.*

3. But they who exalted themselves were both cast down, yet the man more gently, for his judge was the one who orders all things by weight and measure.* The angel was punished, even damned, in fury, but the man only suffered displeasure, not fury. 'For though he was angry, he remembered his mercy.'* For this reason his seed are called the children of wrath,* not of fury, until this day.* If I were not born a child of wrath, I should not have needed to be re-born in baptism;* if I were a child of fury, either

Jn 5:20

2 Cor 10:5

Ps 72:20

Ps 6:1

Ps 35:5

Gen 3:5

Is 14:14

Gal 6:3

Ws 11:21

Hab 3:2
Eph 2:3
1 Sam 5:5

Cf. Jn 3:7

I could not have attained to it, or it would not
have benefitted me. Would you wish to see a
child of fury? If you have seen Satan falling as
Lk 10:18 lightning from heaven,* cast down by the
force of God's fury, you know what the fury
Cf. Ps 97:3, of God is. He did not remember his mercy*
108:6 then, whereas when he is angry he will
Hab 3:2 remember it.* It is not so when his fury is
Cf. Jdt 5:2 kindled.* Woe to the children of disobedi-
Eph 5:6 ence,* to those descended from Adam, who
Eph 2:3 were born of wrath,* but turned it into fury
against themselves by their fiendish obsti-
nacy, turning as it were a switch into a rod—
or rather into a hammer! 'For they store up
Rom 2:5 wrath for themselves in the day of wrath.'*
But what is stored-up wrath but fury? They
have committed the devil's sin, and incur the
same punishment as the devil. Woe too, though
less terrible, to those children of wrath who,
being born in wrath, have not looked forward
to being reborn in grace. For they have died as
they were born, and shall remain children of
wrath. I say of wrath, not of fury, because piety and compassion lead us to believe that
those who are infected by sin from outside
themselves incur the mildest of punishments.

4. Therefore the devil is judged in fury,
Ps 35:3 because his wickedness incurred hatred,* while
that of men incurred wrath, and so is chas-
Cf. Ps 6:2, 37:2 tised in wrath.* Thus all pride is destroyed,
both that which exalts a man and that which
casts him down, for the Father is exceed-
ingly zealous for his son. And in both
instances the Son is dishonored: in the first
because power is usurped in opposition to the
might of God, which is himself, and in the

second because knowledge is presumed not in
accordance with the wisdom of God,* which
is also he. Lord, who is like you?* Who but
your own image, the splendor and likeness of
your being.* He alone is in your form, he
alone did not think it robbery to be equal
with you,* he, the most high Son of the Most
High.* How can he be other than equal with
you? For you and he are one.* His seat is at
your right hand, not under your feet.* How
can anyone presume to usurp the position of
your only begotten Son? Let such a one be
cast down. Is he to take his seat on high?* Let
the chair of pestilence be overturned. Who
shall teach man wisdom?* Is it not you, O
Key of David. Who open and shut to whom-
ever you wish?* How can the doors of the
treasure of wisdom and knowledge be opened
without a key?* How could an entry be
forced? He who does not enter by the door is
a thief and a robber.* Peter, of course, will
enter, for he received the keys.* But he will
not be alone, for he will admit me also, if he
sees fit, and shut out someone else if he sees
fit, through the knowledge and the power
conferred on him from above.*

5. And what are these keys? They are the
power of opening and closing* and of discerning who should be let in and who should be
kept out. They are not in the possession of
the serpent,* but of Christ. Therefore the serpent could not give knowledge which he did
not possess but he who possessed it gave it.
Nor could he have power which he had not
received; it was he who received it, who had
it. Christ it was who gave it, Peter who

Cf. 1 Cor 1:24

Ps 88:9

Col 1:15, Heb 1:3

Ph 2:6

Lk 1:32

Jn 17:22

Ps 109:1

Ps 67:8

Ps 93:10

Rev 3:7

Col 2:3

Jn 10:1

Mt 16:19

Jn 19:11

Rev 11:6

Cf. Col 2:3

received it. He was not puffed up at his knowledge;* nor did he deserve to be cast down because of his power. Why was this? It was because he did not exalt himself against the knowledge of God,* nor did he lay claim to any of those things beyond the knowledge of God, as did he who acted deceitfully in the sight of God, whose wickedness became hateful.* How indeed could Peter have claimed anything beyond the knowledge of God when he described himself as an apostle of Jesus Christ, according to the foreknowledge of God the Father?* And these things were said with reference to the zeal of God which he directed against those who transgressed—whether angel or man, for he found wickedness in both*—just as he destroyed in his furious anger all pride which sets itself up against the knowledge of God.*

III. 6. We must now turn to the zeal of pity—not the zeal directed against us, but that which is extended towards us. For the zeal directed against us, as we have seen, is the zeal of judgement, and has inspired us with sufficient fear from the examples already quoted of those who have received so terrible a punishment. Therefore I will flee from the sight of the anger of the Lord* and go to a place of refuge, to that zeal of mercy which burns sweetly and wholly purifies. Does not charity make amends? Truly it does powerfully. I have read that it covers a multitude of sins.* But I would ask this: is it not right and sufficient to cast down and humble all pride of eyes and heart?* Yes indeed, for love does not vaunt itself and is not puffed up.*

1 Cor 8:1

2 Cor 10:5

Ps 35:3

1 Pet 1:1-2

Job 4:18

2 Cor 10:5

Jer 4:26

1 Pet 4:8

Si 23:5
1 Cor 13:4

Therefore if Our Lord Jesus condescends to come to me, or rather enter into me, not in the zeal of anger or even in wrath, but in love and in a spirit of gentleness,* striving with me   *1 Cor 4:21* with the striving of God*—for what greater at-   *2 Cor 11:2* tribute of God is there than charity?* Then he   *1 Jn 4:16* is indeed God. If he comes in such a spirit, then I know that he is not alone but that the Fa- ther is with him.* What could be more like a   *Jn 16:32* father? Therefore he is not only called the Father of the Word, but the Father of mer- cies,* because it is his nature always to have   *2 Cor 1:3* mercy and to pardon. If I feel that my eyes are opened to understand the Scriptures,* so   *Lk 24:45* that I am enlightened from above to preach the word of wisdom from the heart* or reveal   *1 Cor 12:8* the mysteries of God, or if riches from on high are showered upon me so that in my soul fruits of meditation are produced, I have no doubt that the Bridegroom is with me. For these are gifts of the Word, and it is of his fulness that we have received these gifts.* Again if I am filled with a feeling of   *Jn 1:16* humility rich with devotion whereby love of the truth I have received produces in me so urgent a hatred and contempt for vanity that I cannot be inflamed with pride* by reason   *1 Cor 8:1* of knowledge, nor elated by the frequency of heavenly visitations* then truly I am aware of   *2 Cor 12:7* fatherly activity and do not doubt the Fa- ther's presence. But if I continue as far as I can to respond to this condescension in worthy disposition and action, and the grace of God in me has not been fruitless,* then   *1 Cor 15:10* the Father will make his abode with me* to   *Jn 14:23* nourish me, as the Son will teach me.

7. Consider how great is the grace of intimacy which results from this encounter of the soul and the Word, and how great the confidence which follows this intimacy! I think such a soul need not fear to say, 'My beloved is mine';* for she perceives that she loves, and loves ardently, and has no doubt that she is loved ardently in return. Then by virtue of the single-minded devotion of watchfulness, the care and attention, the diligence and zeal with which she has ceaselessly and ardently studied to please God,* she recognizes these attributes in him also, with certainty and peace, recalling his promise 'with what measure you measure it shall be measured out to you in return'.* Yet the Bride is prudent and careful to take as her share only thankfulness for grace received, for she knows that the initiative lies with the Bridegroom. Thus it is that she mentions his part first: 'My beloved is mine and I am his.'* She knows then without any doubt, from the attributes which have their origin in God, that she who loves is herself loved. And so it is: the love of God gives birth to the love of the soul for God, and his surpassing affection fills the soul with affection, and his concern evokes concern. For when the soul can once perceive the glory of God without a veil,* it is compelled by some affinity of nature to be conformed to it, and be transformed to its very image. So God must appear to you as you have appeared to God; 'with the holy he will be holy, and with an innocent man he will be innocent.'* Why not also loving with the loving, eager with the eager, and concerned with

Sg 2:16

1 Cor 7:32

Mt 7:2

Sg 2:16

2 Cor 3:18

Ps 17:26

those who are concerned?

8. Lastly, he says, 'I love those who love me and they who seek me early shall find me'.* See how he assures you of his love, if *Prov 8:17* you love him, and of his concern for you, if he sees you concerned for him. Do you keep watch? He keeps watch also. If you rise at night before the time of vigil* and hasten to *Lam 2:19* anticipate the morning watch,* you will find *Ps 76:5* him there. He will always be waiting for you. You would be very rash if you claimed to love him first or love him more; his love is greater, and it preceded yours. If the soul knows this— or because she knows it—is it any wonder that this soul, this bride, boasts that that great majesty cares for her alone as though he had no others to care for, and she sets aside all her cares and devotes herself to him alone with all her heart. I must bring this sermon to an end, but I will say one thing to the spiritual among you, a strange thing, but true. The soul which looks on God sees him as though she alone were looked on by him. It is in this confidence that she says he is concerned for her, and she for him, and she sees nothing but herself and him. How good you are, Lord, to the soul who seeks you.* You come to meet *Lam 3:25* her, you embrace her, you acknowledge yourself to be her bridegroom,* you who are the *Rom 9:5* Lord, God blessed for ever above all things.

SERMON SEVENTY

I. HOW THE BRIDEGROOM BECAME THE
BELOVED, AND OF HIS FEEDING AMONG
THE LILIES. II. OF THE SPIRITUAL
LILIES AMONG WHICH THE BRIDEGROOM
FEEDS. III. HOW TRUTH IS RIGHTLY
COMPARED TO A LILY; AND HOW GEN-
TLENESS AND RIGHTEOUSNESS ARE AL-
SO LILIES. IV. HOW ALL THE BRIDE-
GROOM'S ATTRIBUTES ARE LILIES; THE
LILIES POSSESSED BY THE BRIDE-
GROOM'S FRIENDS, AND HOW TWO
LILIES AT LEAST ARE NECESSARY TO
SALVATION.

Sg 2:16

I. 1. **M**Y BELOVED is mine and I am his; he feeds among the lilies.* Who would now accuse the Bride of presumption or insolence, if she says that she is admitted into the company of him who feeds among the lilies? Even if she said he fed among the stars, the very fact that he is said to feed would make it seem a very ordinary thing to enjoy his friendship, for the act of feeding sounds a commonplace and humble thing. And when she says he feeds among the lilies she introduces a note of abasement which takes away and dispels any accusation of presumption. For what are lilies? According

36

to the word of God they are 'the grass of the
fields which today is and tomorrow is thrown
into the oven.'* What then is he who feeds
on grass like a lamb or a calf?* He must be a
lamb* or a fatted calf!† But you may have
been sufficiently alert to notice that the lilies
are mentioned not as his food, but as his place
of feeding: he feeds among the lilies, not on
them. That is the point. He does not eat grass
like an ox,* but walks in the grass, lies down
on the grass* like one of the herd; and what
claim to greatness can there be in that? What
glory can there be for the Bride to have as
her beloved someone who acts like this? To
take it literally then, the modesty of the Bride
and her prudence are shown in her speech, as
she directs her words with judgment* and
tempers the glory of her state by the modesty of her speech.

2. Nevertheless she knows that he who
feeds and he who gives food are one, lingering among the lilies yet reigning above the
stars. But she recalls the humble deeds of her
beloved very willingly because of his humility,
as I said; but even more so because he began
to be her beloved from the time he began to
feed. And not merely from that time but for
that reason, for he who is God above* is the
beloved below; above the stars he reigns and
among the lilies he loves. Even above the stars
he loved because he who is love can never anywhere do other than love. But until he came
down to the lilies and revealed himself feeding among the lilies his love was not returned
and he did not become the beloved.* 'But,'
you say, 'was he not loved by the patriarchs

Mt 6:30

Cf. Is 1:11
*Jn 1:29
†Lk 15:23

Job 40:10
Mt 14:19

Ps 111:5

Lk 2:16

Wis 4:10

and prophets?' Yes, but not until he was seen by them feeding among the lilies. You must admit that they saw him whom they foresaw, unless, that is, you are so lacking in perception as to maintain that one who sees in the spirit sees nothing. Why were they called seers* (for the prophets were thus called) if they saw nothing? Surely because they desired to see him although they did not actually do so,* but they could not desire to see him in the flesh* if they had not seen him in the spirit.* Were all those who wished to see him prophets,* then, or did they all have faith? Those who saw were either prophets or followers of the prophets. To have believed is to have seen. Not only is it possible for him who sees by a spirit of prophecy,* but also for him who sees by faith. And if a man claims to see in the spirit, I think he may well be right.

3. So he who gives food to all has deigned to come down to the lilies and feed among them, and thus become the Beloved,* for he could not be beloved before he was recognized. And when the Bride mentions the beloved, she points this out as the cause of her love for him and her recognition of him.

II. We must find refreshment in the spiritual meaning among the lilies; to understand it physically would be nonsense. We must show, as far as we can, what these spiritual lilies are. We must describe, I think, what the beloved feeds on among the lilies, whether it is the lilies themselves or other plants or flowers hidden among the lilies. This appears some-

1 Sam 9:9

Lk 10:24
Rom 10:18-19
1 Cor 12:29
Cf. Lk 10:24

Rev 19:10

Wis 4:10

what difficult because he is described as feeding himself, not others. Now without doubt he does feed others; anything else would be unworthy of him, but to say that he feeds himself smacks of insufficiency and this cannot be stated of him even in a spiritual sense without lessening his majesty. I do not remember having yet called your attention to the fact that he is mentioned in the Canticle as taking food, although you will remember, I think, that he is mentioned as pasturing the flock. The Bride asked him to show her where he pastured his flock and made them lie down at noon.* Now she describes him as taking food, which she has not mentioned before, but she does not now ask him to show her the place, but indicates it herself, saying expressly that it is among the lilies. She knows this now although she did not know before, because she cannot be equally familiar with what is lofty in the heights and what is lowly on earth. It is a lofty matter, and its place is lofty, and not even the Bride has yet been permitted to approach it.

Sg 1:6

4. Therefore he who feeds his flocks, the shepherd of all, laid aside his glory,* even taking food himself; he is found among the lilies. There he is seen and deeply loved by the Church, poor as he is poor, and, being like her in this, he becomes the Beloved;* and not for this reason alone but because of his truth, mercy and justice;* because in him the promises are fulfilled, iniquities are pardoned.* The arrogant demons are judged, along with the prince of demons. Such then he appeared, worthy of being loved, true in himself, but

Ph 2:7

Wis 4:10

Ps 44:5
Ps 31:1

gentle and just to men. Truly worthy to be
loved and embraced from the depths of men's
hearts! How can the Church hesitate to trust
herself completely to one so faithful to his
word, so ready to forgive, so just in defending? The psalmist had foretold this, saying:

Ps 44:5   'Go forth in splendor and beauty to reign.'*
Whence is this splendor and beauty? From the
lilies, I think. Has anything more splendor
than a lily? Likewise, nothing is lovelier
than the Bridegroom. What then are these

Ps 49:2   lilies from which comes this glorious beauty.*
Ps 44:5   'Ride on to reign in truth, mercy and justice.'*
These are the lilies—the lilies which spring
from the earth, blooming brightly, fairer than
all the flowers on earth, sweeter than the
sweetest perfumes. So the Bridegroom is
among the lilies and it is thus that he is altogether lovely and handsome. Otherwise, seen
in the frailty of flesh, he has no form or

Is 53:2   comeliness.*

5. Glorious among lilies is truth, radiant to
behold, and very fragrant; its radiance and the

Wis 7:26   radiance of the Eternal Light,* the splendor &
Heb 1:3   the figure of God's substance.* It is clearly a lily which our earth brought forth for a new be-
nediction, and prepared before the face of all

Lk 2:31-2   people, a light to lighten the Gentiles.* As long
as the earth lay under a curse, it brought forth

Gen 3:18   thorns and thistles.* But now truth has sprung
Ps 84:12   from the earth* by the Lord's blessing, the
Sg 2:1   flower of the field and the lily of the valley.*
Recognize the lily by its radiance, which shone
in the night for the shepherds when it first
bloomed, for the Gospel says that the Angel of
the Lord stood before them & the brightness

of the Lord shone round about them.* Truly
the Lord's radiance, because it was not that of
an angel, but that of the lily. The angel was
present, certainly, but it was the lily which
shone, even from Bethlehem. Recognize the lily by its fragrance, by which it made itself
known to the Magi* when they were far away.
The star did indeed appear, but the Wise Men
would not have followed it had they not been
drawn by the secret sweetness of the lily's
bloom. Truth is indeed a lily whose fragrance
awakens faith, whose splendor enlightens
the mind.

III. Lift your eyes* to the very person of the
Lord who says in the Gospel, 'I am the
Truth,'* and see how fitly truth may be compared to a lily. Observe, if you have not
already done so, the golden stamens springing
from the centre of the flower, arranged with
beautiful regularity in the form of a crown
and surrounded by the white petals. Now
recognize in Christ the gold of divinity
crowned with the purity of his human nature,
that is Christ wearing the diadem with which
his mother crowned him.* For when he wears
the diadem with which his father crowned him
he dwells in light inaccessible,* and you cannot yet see him thus. But I will speak of this
another time.

6. Truth, then, is a lily; so is clemency.
Well may clemency be called a lily, for it has
the whiteness of innocence and the fragrance
of hope, 'for for a man of peace life yet
remains.'* The clement man has a good
hope;* even in this present life he is a shining

Lk 2:9

Mt 2:7

Gen 13:14

Jn 14:6

Sg 3:11

1 Tim 6:16

Ps 36:37

Wis 12:19

example of fellowship. Does not the lily give off the fragrance of hope as well as the brightness of courtesy? Surely clemency, as well as truth, springs from the earth?*. Just so the Lamb, who is the ruler of the earth,* springs from the earth—that Lamb who was led to the slaughter and opened not his mouth.*

Clemency and truth, then, spring from the earth, as does righteousness,* for the prophet Isaiah says, 'Shower, ye heavens, from above, and let the skies rain down righteousness; let the earth open and bring forth a Saviour, and let righteousness arise with him.'* You know from Scripture that righteousness is a lily, for 'the just man shall grow as the lily and blossom for ever before the Lord'.* This is not the lily which today is and tomorrow is cast into the oven;* it will blossom for ever. And it will blossom before the Lord, for the righteous man shall be held in everlasting remembrance, and shall not be afraid of evil tidings,* that is, the tidings by which sinners are commanded to go into the furnace of fire.* The radiance of this lily shines on all except on those who take no pleasure in it. It is the sun, but not the sun which rises on the evil and the good,* for those who shall say, 'The sun of righteousness has not risen upon us,'* have never seen his light. Those who have seen it are those who say, 'Upon you who fear God the sun of righteousness will arise'.* So the radiance of this lily is for the righteous, but its fragrance reaches even the wicked, though not for their good. We hear the righteous saying, 'We are the goodly fragrance of Christ in every place,* but to some a fragrance of life

Ps 84:12
Is 16:1

Is 53:7

Ps 84:10

Is 45:8

Hos 14:6

Mt 6:30

Ps 111:7

Ps 20:10

Mt 5:45

Wis 5:6

Mal 4:2

2 Cor 2:14-15

leading to life, to others a fragrance of death leading to death'. Who, even the very wicked, does not approve the sentiments of the righteous,* even though he may not like his actions? Happy is he who has no reason to judge himself for what he approves. For a man judges himself if he approves the good but does not love it; he is not happy but wretched, being condemned by his own judgment.* Who is more wretched than a man for whom the fragrance of life is the harbinger not of life but of death?* Or perhaps its bearer rather than its harbinger.

Rom 14:22

Tt 3:11

Prov 16:14

IV. 7. The Bridegroom has many other lilies in his garden besides those the prophet has mentioned to us: truth, clemency, and righteousness.* It will not be difficult for each of you to find other such lilies in the garden of so delightful a Bridegroom. It is full and overflowing with them; who can count them? There are as many lilies as there are virtues, and there is no end to virtues with the Lord of virtues.* If the fulness of virtues is in Christ, so too is the fulness of lilies. Perhaps he called himself a lily because he is wholly surrounded by lilies, and all the events of his life are lilies: his conception, birth, way of life, teaching, the miracles he did, the sacraments he ordained, his passion and death, his resurrection and ascension. Which of these are not radiant and sweetly fragrant? At his conception there streamed from the fulness of the overshadowing spirit* a shaft of heavenly brightness so blinding that not even the holy Virgin could have endured it had not the

Ps 44:5

Ps 23:10

Lk 1:35

power of the Spirit given her shade. His birth radiated through the undefiled purity of his mother; his life was aflame with innocence, his teaching with truth, his miracles with purity of heart, his sacraments with the hidden power of his goodness;* his passion shone with his acceptance of suffering, his death with the freedom he had to avoid death, his resurrection with the radiance which gave fortitude to the martyrs, his ascension with the glory of promises fulfilled. How goodly also is the fragrance of faith in all these mysteries—that faith is ours, and fills our hearts and minds, although we have not seen their radiance. 'Blessed are those who have not seen, yet have believed.'* May my part in these be the fragrance of life which proceeds from them. It is by means of faith that I breathe in their fragrance; indeed, their number is so great that they lighten the burden of my exile, and ever renew in my heart the longing for my true home.*

8. The friends of the bridegroom have lilies too, but not in great numbers. For they have all received the Spirit in their measure, and in their measure also virtues and gifts,* but he alone possesses the Spirit without measure who possesses it fully. It is one thing to possess lilies, and another to have nothing but lilies. Whom can you show me among the sons of captivity* so blameless and so holy that he can fill all his land with flowers—and with flowers such as these? Not even a child a day old is without stain upon earth.* A man is great is he can grow even three or four lilies on his land among the thickets of thorns and

Margin references:
1 Tim 3:16
Jn 20:29
Ps 50:12
Cf. Jn 3:34
Dan 5:13; 6:13
Job 14:4 (LXX)

thistles, which are the deep-rooted seeds of
the ancient curse.* For myself, poor as I am,
I am well pleased if I can clear my little plot
of earth by uprooting and banishing this evil
crop of unrighteousness and wickedness sufficiently to grow even one lily, so that he who
feeds among the lilies may sometimes see fit
to feed with me.

Gen 3:18

9. I said 'one', but my mouth spoke out
of the poverty of my heart.* One will indeed
be insufficient; at least two are necessary. I
refer to self-control and innocence; the one
without the other will not save us. It will be
vain for me to invite the Bridegroom to come
to either of these, for he is said to feed among
the lilies, not to feed on one lily. So I will take
pains to have more than one lily, so that he
who would feed among the lilies shall not
find fault with his servant* for having only
one lily, and turn away in displeasure. So I
must put innocence first, and if I can join self-
control to it I shall consider myself rich in the
possession of my lilies.* But if I can add a
third to these—patience—I shall be a king. It
could be that the two would suffice, but in
times of temptation they might not be
enough, for the life of man on earth is a
battle with temptation,* and patience is
necessary, the nurse and guardian of both.
And if the lover of lilies should come and
find these three,* I am sure that he will not
scorn to feed with us, and eat the Passover
with us;* for he will find great sweetness in
the first two, and in the third there is great
protection.

Lk 6:45

Ps 26:9

cf. Gen 13:2

Job 17:1

Lk 12:43

Mt 26:18

We shall see later how he who gives food to

all is said to feed. But now it is clear that not
only does the Bridegroom appear among the
lilies, but he cannot be found anywhere else,
since even part of him is a lily, and he is himself a lily, the Bridegroom of the Church,
Jesus Christ our Lord, who is above all,

Rom 9:5   blessed for ever.* Amen.

SERMON SEVENTY-ONE

I. IN WHAT CONSISTS THE BRIGHTNESS
AND FRAGRANCE OF THE LILY, WHICH
IS VIRTUE. II. WHEREIN LIES THE
BRIGHTNESS OF THE SOUL, AND HOW
THE BRIDEGROOM BOTH FEEDS AMONG
THE LILIES AND GIVES FOOD. III. HOW
GOD IS FED BY MEN AND MEN BY GOD,
AND OF THE DIFFERENT KINDS OF UNITY
BY WHICH THE FATHER AND THE SON
ARE ONE, AND GOD AND MAN ARE ONE
SPIRIT. IV. OF THE UNITY OF SUB-
STANCE OF THE FATHER AND THE SON,
AND THE ACCORD OF GOD AND MAN,
AND HOW MAN ABIDES IN GOD FROM
ALL ETERNITY, BUT NOT GOD IN MAN.
V. A THIRD EXPLANATION OF THE FEED-
ING OF THE BRIDEGROOM, WHO IS THE
WORD OF GOD, AND HOW HE DOES NOT
FEED UPON GOOD WORKS, WHICH ARE
NOT FOUND AMONG THE VIRTUES, THAT
IS, AMONG LILIES.

I. 1. THE END of the last sermon shall be this one's beginning. The Bridegroom, then, is a lily, but not a lily among thorns,* for he who has no sin has no thorns.* It is the Bride he describes as a lily among thorns,* for if she

Sg 2:2
1 Pet 2:22
Sg 2:2

47

said that she had no thorn, she would be deceiving herself, and the truth would not be in her.* Now he has declared that he is a flower and a lily, but not among thorns; indeed he says, 'I am the rose of Sharon and the lily of the valley'.* There is no mention of thorns, because he alone among men has no need to say, 'I writhe in anguish, and a thorn pierces me.'* Therefore he is never without lilies, and always without faults, because he is always radiant and fairer than the children of men.* You then who hear or read these words,[1] take care to have lilies in your soul, if you wish to have him who dwells among the lilies dwelling in you. Let the radiance and fragrance of your character show that your actions, your endeavors and your desires are lilies. For characters have their own color and fragrance, and souls have their own distinctive color and fragrance just as bodies do. Now their color is derived from conscience, and their fragrance from reputation. 'You have made our odor hateful to Pharaoh and his servants.'* they say, referring to reputation. Then the intention of the heart and the judgment of the conscience gives its color to your action. Vices are black and virtue is white, and the awakened conscience distinguishes between them. When the Lord speaks of the good eye & the faulty eye* he makes the same distinction, for there is as great a difference between white and black as between light and darkness.* Therefore what proceeds from a pure

1 Jn 1:8

Sg 2:1

Ps 31:4

Ps 45:3

Ex 5:21

Mt 6:22-23

Gen 1:4

---

1. On whether the sermons were designed to the preached or read, see Jean Leclercq, Introduction to *Bernard of Clairvaux: On the Song of Songs, II;* CF 7:vii-xxx.

heart and a good conscience* is virtue, white
and shining; and if it is followed by a good
report it is a lily too, for it has both color and
fragrance.

2. Even if virtue is not made greater by
good report, it becomes brighter and more
beautiful. If in the intention there is any
blemish, what proceeds from it will not be
free from blemish; for a defect in the root
will appear on the branch.* Consequently
whatever proceeds from a defective root
—be it speech, action, or prayer—may not be
called a lily, even if its fragrance seems to conceal the blemish, for it lacks the bright color.
How can it be a lily when it is disfigured by a
blemish? Reputation cannot compensate for
virtue, when conscience is aware of some
defect. Virtue will be satisfied with the radiance of a good conscience, even when no
fragrance of reputation can follow; but the
fragrance of a good reputation cannot compensate for the stain of a bad conscience. Yet
a good man will always intend what is good,
not only before God but also in the sight of
men,* that he may truly be a lily.

II. 3. But there is a radiance of soul which
comes from the mercy and forgiveness of
God, as he himself says through the prophet
Isaiah: 'Even if your sins are as scarlet, they
shall be as white as snow; even if they are
blood-red, they shall be as white as snow.'*
And there is a brightness with which a man
clothes himself, when he shows mercy with
cheerfulness;* if you look at a man whom the
Psalmist describes as happy, a man who

1 Tim 1:5

Rom 11:16

Rom 12:17

Is 1:18

Rom 12:8

Ps 111:8
shows mercy and lends,* do you not see that
his joyfulness of spirit begets a radiance in his
2 Cor 9:7
face and his deeds?* But the face and deeds
of a man who gives reluctant and grudging
service are not radiant, but dark and gloomy.
Ibid.
That is why the Lord loves a cheerful giver.*
How could he love a gloomy one? He looked
favourably upon Abel because of his radiant
Gen 4:4-5
gladness, but turned away from Cain* because Cain's face was heavy, no doubt with
sadness and envy. Consider what the color of
sadness and jealousy must be like, for God to
turn away his face from it. There is a beautiful and sensitive description of the radiant joy
which lights up kindness in the writings of the
*Ovid, Metamor-
phoses 8.677-688
poet: 'The joyful of countenance have overcome all things.'* The Lord loves not only a
Rom 12:8
cheerful giver† but one who gives with simplicity. Simplicity also is radiance. We prove this
from its contrary: duplicity is a blemish; I
say more, it is a disfigurement. For what is
duplicity but deception? But as for the person who practises deception in the sight of
Ps 35:2
God, his wickedness is found out and hated.*
Indeed, 'Blessed is the man to whom the Lord
imputes no sin, and in whose spirit there is no
Ps 31:2
guile.'* The Lord described these disfigure-
ments—deception and gloominess—when he
Mt 6:16
said, 'Do not be gloomy, like the hypocrites'.*
The Bridegroom, being himself virtue, takes
1 Cor 1:24
pleasure in virtues;* being himself a lily, he a-
bides willingly among the lilies; being himself
Wis 7:26
radiance, he delights in their radiance.*

4. Perhaps it is because he delights in the
radiance and fragrance of virtues that he is
said to feed among the lilies. In the days of his

earthly life he fed at the house of Martha
and Mary* and took his rest physically among
the lilies—for those I speak of were lilies—and
likewise he refreshed his spirit with their
devotion and virtues.* If at that hour a
prophet had entered, or an angel or any other
spiritual being, knowing what majesty was
reclining there, would he not have been
amazed at the condescension and kindness
which they saw him show to those of pure
souls and chaste bodies, although they were
of earthly body and belonged to the weaker
sex? Would they not have given testimony,
saying, 'I saw him not only abiding, but feeding, among the lilies.' The Bridegroom was
found feeding flesh and spirit among the
lilies, I say. But I think that he was giving
them food, of a spiritual kind. He fed them
in the same way as he himself was fed. In the
same way he comforted the fearfulness of the
women, cheered their humility, and enriched
their devotion. You have seen that 'For him,
to be nourished is to nourish'. Now see how
the converse is true, and to nourish is to be
nourished. 'Lord, you have fed me from my
youth', says the holy patriarch Jacob.* He
is the good householder, who provides for his
family,* especially in bad times,† so that he
may give them food in times of hunger,*
feeding them with the bread of life* and
understanding, and so he brings them to
eternal life. But as he feeds them, he is himself
also fed, and fed with the food which he takes
most gladly,* that is our progress. 'The joy of
the Lord is our strength.'*

    5. So it is that while he feeds others he is

Lk 10:38

Jdg 15:19

Gen 48:15

*1 Tim 5:8
†Ps 93:13
*Ps 32:19
Si 15:3

Gen 27:9
Neh 8:10

himself fed, and while he refreshes us with spiritual joy he himself joys in our spiritual progress. My penitence, my salvation, are his food. I myself am his food. Does he not eat ashes as though they were bread?* For I as a sinner;* it is I who am the ashes† to be eaten by him. I am chewed as I am reproved by him; I am swallowed as I am taught; I am digested as I am changed; I am assimilated as I am transformed; I am made one as I am conformed. Do not wonder at this,* for he feeds upon us and is fed by us that we may be the more closely bound to him. Otherwise we are not perfectly united with him. For if I eat and am not eaten, then he is in me but I am not yet in him.* But if I am eaten and do not eat, then he has me in him, but it would appear he is not yet in me; and in neither case will there be perfect union between us. But he eats me that he may have me in himself, and he in turn is eaten by me that he may be in me, and the bond between us will be strong and the union complete, for I shall be in him and he will likewise be in me.

6. Shall I show you my meaning by a comparison? Lift your eyes* then to a loftier aspect, which nevertheless has much in common with this one. If the Bridegroom himself were in the Father in such a way that the Father was not in him, or the Father in him in such a way that he was not in the Father, then I would say that the unity between them would be less than perfect, if indeed it were a unity. But since he is in the Father and the Father in him, nothing cripples their unity, but he and the Father are truly one.*

Ps 110:10
*Lk 5:8
†Gen 18:27

Jn 5:28

Cf. Jn 6:57

Gen 43:29

Jn 10:38, 30

Thus the soul which finds its good in cleaving
to God* will not consider itself perfectly   *Ps 72:28*
united with him until it perceives that he
abides in her and she in him. Not even then
may she be said to be one with God as the
Father and Son are one, although 'he who
cleaves to God is one spirit with him'.* This I   *Cf. 1 Cor 6:17*
have read; the other I have not. I am not
speaking of myself. I am nothing;* but surely   *1 Cor 13:2*
no-one in his senses, either on earth or in
heaven, would appropriate to himself that
utterance of the Only-begotten Son: 'I and
the Father are one'.* Yet I, though dust and   *Jn 10:30*
ashes,* relying on the words of Scripture, am   *Gn 18:27*
not afraid to say that I am one spirit* with   *1 Cor 6:17*
God, if ever I shall have been convinced by
sure experience that I cleave to God, after
the manner of those who abide in charity,
and therefore abide in God and God in
them,* feeding somehow upon God, and   *1 Jn 4:16*
being fed by God. For I think that it was
about such a union that it was said, 'he who
cleaves to God is one spirit with him.'* So   *1 Cor 6:17*
what? The Son says, 'I am in the Father
and the Father in me,* and we are one'.† Man   **Jn 10:38*
says, 'I am in God, and God is in me, and we   *†Jn 10:30*
are one spirit'.

7. But do the Father and the Son not feed
upon each other, that they may be in each
other, just as God and man, by feeding
mutually upon each other, abide as one
spirit even though they are not one? Not so;
for they do not indwell the one the other in
the same way, nor is their unity the same.[1]
For the Father and the Son are in one
another, they are, in a not only ineffable but

incomprehensible way, capable equally of containing and of being contained, but capable of containing each other without being divisible, and of being contained without being divided. For as the Church sings in a hymn:

Ambrose,
Splendor Paternae
Gloriae; *PL 16:*
1411.

'The Word in God the Father one,
The Father perfect in the Son.'*

Mt 17:5

The Father is in the Son in whom he is well pleased,* and the Son is in the Father from whom he has never been separated, just as there has never been a time when he was not begotten. Now through charity man is in God and God in man; for St John says 'He who dwells in charity dwells in God and God in him'.* This is the harmony by which they are two in one spirit,* or indeed are one spirit.† Do you see the distinction? For to be of the same substance is not the same as to be of the same will.* If you consider the matter, their difference in unity is indicated by the words *unum* and *unus,* for *unus,* one person, cannot be applied to the Father and to the Son, nor *unum,* one substance, to man and to God. The Father & Son cannot be said to be one person, because the Father is one and the Son is one. Yet they are said to be, and they are, one, because they have & are one substance, since they have not each separate substance. On the contrary, since God and man do not share the same nature or substance, they cannot be said to be a unity, yet they are with complete truth & accuracy, said to be one spirit, if they cohere with the bond of love. But that unity is caused not so much by the identity of essences as by the concurrence of wills.

1 Jn 4:16
*Gen 2:26
†1 Cor 6:17

consubstantiale et
consentibile

9. Now if I am not mistaken, not only

the difference of kind but also the difference
of degree in these unities is clear enough; for
the one exists in one mode of being and the
other between different modes. What can be
as different as the unity of one being and the
unity of more than one? For as I have said,
the expressions *unus* and *unum* indicate the
distinction between the types of unity, for
unum denotes that the unity of the Father
and the Son is one of essence, while *unus*
denotes not that, but the concurrence of
wills in charity.* Nevertheless by an exten-
sion of meaning the Father and the Son can
truly be said to be *unus,* one, in that there is
one God, one Lord,* and there are other
characteristics which may be attributed to
each and not to one in particular. For their
Godhead, their majesty, is no more distinct
than their substance or their nature or mode
of being. And all these things, if considered
rightly, are not diverse or divided in one and
the other but are *unum.*

IV. I have said too little. They are *unum*
with one other also. What of that unity in
which we read that many hearts and souls
are one?* They are not, I think, to be considered as a true unity compared to this one,
which does not unite many, but signifies one
uniquely. Therefore since that unity is not
brought about by the act of uniting, but
exists from all eternity, it is unique and
supreme, nor is it brought about by that
spiritual feeding which I have spoken of, since
it has no cause, but has existence.* Even less
should it be thought of as brought about by

consentanea
quaedam affec-
tionum pietas

1 Cor 8:6

Ac 4:32

quia nec fit;
est enim

some conjunction of essences or some agreement of wills since there are none of these. There is in them, as has been said, one essence and one will, and where there is only one, there can be no agreement or combining or incorporation or anything of that kind. For there must be at least two wills for there to be agreement, and two essences for there to be combining or uniting in agreement. There are none of these things in the Father and the Son since they have neither two essences nor two wills. In them each of these things are one,* or rather, as I remember saying before, these two things are one (*unum*) in them and one with them, and thus, as they abide in each other in a way beyond comprehension or comparison, they are truly and uniquely one.* But if anyone would affirm that there is agreement between the Father and the Son, I do not contest it provided that it is understood that there is not a union of wills but a unity of will.

10. But we think of God and man as dwelling in each other in a very different way, because their wills, and their substances are distinct and different; that is, their substances are not intermingled, yet their wills are in agreement; and this union is for them a communion of wills and an agreement in charity. Happy is this union if you experience it, but compared with the other, it is no union at all.

There is a saying by one who experienced it, 'For me it is good to cleave to God.'* Good indeed, if you cleave wholly to him. Who is there who cleaves perfectly to God,*

una

Jn 10:30, 17:22

Ps 72:28

1 Cor 6:17

unless he who, dwelling in God, is loved by God* and, reciprocating that love, draws God into himself. Therefore, when God and man cleave wholly to each other—it is when they are incorporated* into each other by mutual love that they cleave wholly to each other—I would say beyond all doubt that God is in man and man in God. Yet man truly abides in God from all eternity, for he is loved from all eternity, if he is one of those who say that God loved us and accepted us* in his beloved Son before the foundation of the world; and God truly abides in man, when he is loved by man. And if this is so, man is indeed in God, even when God is not in man; but God is not in the man who is not in God. For he cannot abide in love* even if he loves for a time yet is unloved. Nor can he yet love, though already loved; otherwise what is the meaning of the saying: 'Since he first loved us'*? But when he who was already loved begins to love, then man is in God and God in man. But the man who does not love has clearly never been loved; it follows that he is not in God nor God in him.* These things have been said to show the difference between the relationship which is the unity of the Father and the Son,* and the one which makes the man who cleaves to God one spirit with him,* lest perhaps when you read that a man abides in love because he abides in God and God in him,* and that the Son is in the Father and the Father in him, you should imagine that the prerogative of the adoptive Son is the same as that of the Only begotten.

1 Jn 4:16, 1 Th 1:4

inviscerati. *Cf. Augustine, Sermo 24.1; PL 38:162.*

Jn 17:24, Eph 1:6

Jn 15:9

1 Jn 4:10

Jn 10:30

1 Cor 6:17

1 Jn 4:16

Jn 10:38

V. 11. Now that we have dealt with these matters, we must return to 'him who feeds among the lilies' because that was where we were when we made this digression. Whether that has been of value you must judge. I had already suggested two explanations of this passage; first, that he who is virtue and radiance* feeds upon the virtue of those on whom his radiance has shone; then, that he receives penitent sinners* in penitence into his body, which is the Church, and that he who never sinned made himself sin* to unite them with himself, so that the body of sin in which the sinners had once been implanted might be destroyed,* and that they might be justified by grace and become righteousness in him.*

12. I would add a third which comes to mind, and I think it will suffice not only for an explanation of this passage but for an end to this sermon: The word of God, the Bridegroom, is truth.* This you know; now hear the rest. When it is heard but not obeyed, it remains empty and, as it were, fruitless, altogether full of sorrow, and complaining that is has been uttered in a void. But do you not see that if it is obeyed the word seems to grow weightier, because deed is added to word, as it is strengthened by the fruits of obedience,* the harvest of righteousness? This is why he says in the Apocalypse, 'Behold I stand at the door and knock, if any man hears my voice and opens the door I will come in to him and will sup with him, and he with me'.* The word of the Lord by the prophet Isaiah seems to give approval to this

1 Cor 1:24, Wis 7:26

Lk 5:32, Col 1:24

2 Cor 5:21, 1 Pet 2:22

Rom 6:6, 5

2 Cor 5:21, Rom 3:24

Jn 17:17

2 Cor 9:10

Rev 3:20

interpretation where he says that his word shall not return to him empty* but shall prosper and accomplish that for which he sent it. 'It shall not return to me empty,' he says, 'but as though prospering in all things* it shall be filled with the good deeds of those who shall obey it in love.'* For in common parlance a word is said to be fulfilled when it has produced its effect; but until it has discharged its task it is meaningless and barren, and somehow starved.

13. But hear how the word declares he is fed: 'My food,' he says, 'is to do the will of my Father.'* This word of the Word shows clearly that doing good is his food, and if he finds it among the lilies it is among the virtues. If any is found outside even if it seems to be in itself good food, he who feeds among the lilies will not touch it. For example, he does not receive alms from the hand of a robber or a usurer, nor indeed from a hypocrite who has a trumpet sounded before him when he gives alms that he may be praised by men.* Nor will he by any means hear the prayer of someone who loves to pray at the street-corners* so as to be seen by men. For the prayers of the sinners will be hateful to him.* The man who knows that his brother has anything against him would offer his gift at the altar in vain.* God would not look upon the sacrifice of Cain* because he did not walk righteously* with his brother. On the evidence of the prophet Isaiah, the sabbaths of the Jews, their new moons, and their sacrifices, were such an abomination to him* that he protested openly that he hated them

Is 55:11

Gen 39:2

Wis 3:9

Jn 4:34

Mt 6:2

Mt 6:5

Prov 28:9

Mt 5:23-24
Gen 4:5
Gal 2:14

Is 1:13

from his soul, and he said, 'When you come to appear before me, who has required this at your hands?'* Those hands, I think lack the fragrance of lilies, and therefore he rejected their gifts. Since he has been used to feeding among the lilies, and not among the thorns,* were their hand not full of thorns to whom he said, 'Your hands are full of blood?'* And the hands of Esau were hairy, as though covered with thorns.* Therefore they were not permitted to wait upon the Holy One.*

14. I fear there may be some among us whose gifts the Bridegroom does not accept because they lack the fragrance of lilies; for if my fasting reflects my own self-will,* it will not be acceptable to him, and he will find no fragrance in my fasting, since its odor is not that of the lily of obedience, but the weed of self-will. And the same thing, I feel, must be true not only of fasting but of silence, vigils, prayer, spiritual reading, manual labor, and indeed of every detail of the monk's life when self-will is found in it instead of obedience to his masters.* Such observances— although good in themselves—are not, I think, to be accounted as among the lilies, that is, among the virtues; but such a man will hear addressed to him the word of the prophet Isaiah: 'Is this the fast that I chose?'* says the Lord. And he will add, 'In the day of your good deeds you will find your pleasures.' Self-will is a great evil and through it your good deeds become not good for you. Therefore such deeds need to become lilies, for he who feeds among the lilies will not taste of anything which is defiled by self-will. Wisdom

Marginal references:
Is 1:12
Sg 2:2
Is 1:15
Gen 27:23
Heb 6:10
Is 58:3-5
Is 58:3, Si 11:27
Wis 8:1

it is who reaches the ends of the world in purity,* and whom no defilement can touch.† Therefore the bridegroom loves to feed among the lilies, that is, among hearts which are pure and undefiled. But how long shall this be? 'Until the day breathes forth life and the shadows lie prostrate.'* This passage is full of obscurities and difficulties; we may not enter the forest of this deep mystery except by the clear light of day. Now, I have talked too long, the day has come to an end* and we unwillingly withdraw from the lilies. I have not been carried away by talking; the fragrance of the flowers would turn aside its weariness. Little* seems to remain of the verse we are considering; but that little is full of mystical meaning, like all the rest of this song, but he who opens the doors to mysteries* will be at hand, I trust, when we knock, and will not shut the mouths of those who speak of him;* for he is more wont to open those which are closed, he who is the Bridegroom of the Church, Jesus Christ Our Lord, who is God above all,* blessed for ever. Amen.

*Wis 8:1
†Wis 7:25

Sg 2:17

Lk 24:29

Jn 16:16

Prov 20:19

Cf. Est 14:9

Rom 9:5

1. ¶7, l. 7. In some editions of sermon 71, two paragraphs of amplification follow here. See SBOp 2:218-219.

SERMON SEVENTY-TWO

I. OF THE WORDS INTRODUCING TWO
PASSAGES: 'UNTIL THE DAY BREATHES
FORTH LIFE' ETC., AND HOW THE BRIDE-
GROOM DOES NOT THEN EAT BUT
DRINKS. OF THE SPIRITUAL DAY AND
SHADOWS, AND HOW WHEN THE DAY
BREATHES FORTH LIFE THEY LIE
PROSTRATE AND ARE DONE AWAY.
III. OF THE DAY WHICH BREATHES,
WHICH INSTILS LIFE, EXPIRES, CON-
SPIRES, RESPIRES, AND SIGHS IN THE
NIGHT. IV. HOW THOSE WHO BREATHE
IN THE DAY LIVE IN ABUNDANCE WHILE
THOSE WHO SIGH BY NIGHT SUFFER
LACK.

'MY BELOVED IS MINE and
I am his; he feeds among the
lilies until the day breathes
forth life and the shadows lie prostrate.*
Only the last clause of this passage has now to
be treated, and I am in doubt, on entering
upon it, as to which of the two preceding ones
it should be joined to, for I cannot connect it
with either. For whether you say 'My beloved
is mine and I am his, until the day breathes
forth life and the shadows lie prostrate'—
putting in parenthesis 'who feeds among the

I. 1.

Sg 2:16-17

62

lilies'—or whether you follow the literal order
'who feeds among the lilies until the day
breathes forth life and the shadows lie prostrate', you will make good sense. The only
difference is that when you join 'until' to
the first clause, you include the other clause
in the meaning; if you join it to the second
you exclude the first clause. If we suppose
that the Bridegroom ceases to feed among the
lilies when day has come to fulness, will he
likewise cease to incline toward the Bride or
she towards him? Not at all. They will continue to do so for ever. The only difference
will be that their relationship will be happier
as it is stronger, and stronger as it is less
hindered. This word 'until' must be understood in its meaning in the Gospel according to Matthew, where it is related that
Joseph did not know Mary 'until she brought
forth her first born son,'* for he did not
know her afterwards. Or as in that verse in
the psalm, 'Our eyes wait for the Lord our
God, until he has mercy upon us':* when he
begins to have mercy they will not turn
away; as Our Lord said to the Apostles, 'I am
with you even unto the end of the world'.*
He will not cease to be with us afterwards.
But now see how it appears if you join the
clause beginning 'until' to 'my beloved is
mine and I am his'. For if you prefer to take
it with 'who feeds among the lilies' you must
understand it in a different sense. Also, it is
more difficult to explain how the beloved
ceases to feed when the day breathes forth
life. Even if it is the day of resurrection, how
will he want to feed less among the lilies when

Mt 1:25

Ps 122:2

Mt 28:20

there is a greater abundance of them? But that
is enough about the connection of the clauses.

2. Now consider with me how the Bridegroom, living and rejoicing in the midst of a
kingdom bright with lilies, is not said to be
feeding as he had previously been accustomed
to do. For where now are the sinners whom
Christ has, as it were, ground and pressed
with the teeth of hard discipline, of mortifi-
cation of the flesh and the heart's contri-

Qo 12:12   tion,* so that he may incorporate them into
himself? But the Bridegroom, the Word, will
no longer require to be fed by any deeds or
words of obedience where the only activity is
repose, and contemplation and affection the
only duty. His food is indeed to do the will of

Jn 4:34   his Father;* but here below, not there. When
all is done, what is there for him to do? And
we know that all will be accomplished. Then
the saints will know what the will of God is,

Rom 12:2   which is good and acceptable, and perfect.*
Surely when perfection is reached, nothing
remains to be done. There remains only to
enjoy it, not to bring it about; to experience
it, not to strive for it; to live by it, not to
carry it out laboriously. For is it not that
very will for whose accomplishment on earth
as in heaven we are taught by the Lord to

Is 54:13, Mt 6:10   pray* with such earnest supplication that the
activity may not weary us, but its fruits may
be our delight? So the Bridegroom, the Word,
will have no need for the food of good works
since all work must needs cease where wisdom
is understood fully by all, for it is said, 'They
who have little need of activity shall under-

Si 38:25   stand it.'*

3. But let us see whether our words can stand alongside the sense in which some interpret the saying that he takes delight in the brightness of virtues; for among the other interpretations we have not missed that one. Shall we say that there will be no virtues, or that the Bridegroom will then take no pleasure in them? Surely either of these is unreasonable. But see whether perhaps he delights in them in some other way—for there is no question that he delights in them—maybe as drink rather than as food. In our life in this world no virtue is so purified or made so sweet and clear that it would be easy for the Bridegroom to drink of it; yet he who desires that all men be saved* overlooks many things, and strives with skill and toil to draw from that which he cannot easily drink something which may be relished as food. There will come a time when virtue need not be pressed wearily by the teeth, or rather cause weariness to the one who eats, but will give pleasure without trouble to the one who drinks, being used as a drink, not as food.* For you have his promise in the Gospel: 'I will not drink of the fruit of the vine, he says, 'until I drink it new with you in my Father's kingdom'.* There is no mention of eating. We read in the prophet: 'Like a strong man drunk with wine', but here* too there is no mention at all of food. The bride then is aware of this mystery when she finds her beloved and sees him among the lilies, and she names a time until when he will deign to do this; or rather she knows and states a time already determined saying, 'until the day

1 Tim 2:4

1 Cor 3:2

Mt 26:29

Ps 77:65

Sg 2:17

breathes forth life and the shadows lie prostrate.* For she knew that he would drink of virtues rather than eat them. This seems to follow the normal custom of taking drink after food. Therefore he who eats now will drink hereafter, and with more pleasure and tranquility, for he will drink what he now partakes of with difficulty.

II. 4. Now let us turn to consider that day and those shadows: what day this is, what shadows these are, how the one breathes forth life, and why the other lies prostrate. For this saying is strange and without parallel: 'until the day breathes forth life'. It is only here, if I am not mistaken, that you will find the day spoken of as 'breathing'. Breezes, not times, are said to breathe. A man breathes, all the other animals breathe; it is the air they ceaselessly breathe which enables their life to continue. And what is this but the wind? The Holy Spirit also breathes; that is why he is spirat...spiritus called 'Spirit', one who breathes.* How then can a day breathe, since it is neither wind, nor spirit, nor animal? Yet it is not merely said to breathe but to breathe forth life. It is no less strange that the shadows are said to lie Sg 2:17 prostrate.* For at the rising of physical, visible light shadows do not lie prostrate but melt away. But the reality must be understood beyond the physical way. If we find a spiritual day and spiritual shadows, perhaps the meaning of the one 'lying prostrate' and of the other 'breathing forth life', will become clearer. Anyone who understands in a literal sense the day of which the prophet said

'One day in your courts is better than thousands',* will take anything in a literal sense. There is also a day with an evil significance* which is cursed by the Prophets. Let us not suppose that the day which the Lord has made is one of those visible days. It must be a day in a spiritual sense.

Ps 83:11

Job 3:3, Jer 20:14

5. Who can doubt that that which overshadowed Mary as she conceived* was a spiritual shadow; so too was that of which the prophet Jeremiah said, 'The Lord's anointed is a spirit before our face, and beneath his shadow shall we live among the heathen'.* But I think that in this passage 'shadows' refer to those hostile powers which the Apostle Paul called not merely shadows or darkness but even the princes of darkness* and that this includes also those from our race who consent with them, children of night, not of light or day,* and when the day breathes forth life these shadows will not be annihilated like natural shadows, which we see not only fading away but completely disappearing; they will not be utterly destroyed but they will be utterly wretched. They will still exist, but cowering and subdued. The Psalm says 'he will cower and fall when he has domination over the poor',* referring no doubt to the prince of darkness. So his nature shall not be destroyed but his power shall be taken away; his substance shall not perish but the hour of darkness* and its power† shall pass. They are taken away that they may not see the glory of God; they are not blotted out, that they may burn for ever.

How shall the shadows not lie prostrate

Lk 1:35

Lam 4:20

Eph 6:12

1 Th 5:5

Ps 9(B):10

*Mic 14:35
†Lk 22:53.

when the mighty are put down from their

Lk 1:52, Ps 109:1 seat and are made a footstool?* That must
soon come to pass. It is the last hour: the
Rev 1:1, 1 Jn 2:18, night is far spent, and the day is at hand.*
Rom 13:12 The day will breathe forth life, the night will
breathe its last. The night is the devil, night is
2 Cor 12:7 the angel of Satan,* though he may disguise
†2 Cor 11:14 himself as an angel of light.† Night is the
Antichrist, whom the Lord shall slay with the
2 Th 2:8 breath of his mouth* and destroy with the
brightness of his coming. Is not the Lord
the day? Clearly he is the day, bright and
throbbing with life. He puts the shadows to
Job 15:30 flight with the breath of his mouth,* and
destroys the phantoms with the brightness of
his coming.

If you prefer to take the words 'to lie
prostrate' in their literal meaning, taking the
view that 'to lie prostrate' means nothing but
to be destroyed, I would accept this interpretation; for the dark sayings and riddles of
the Scriptures we call 'shadows' as we do the
ambiguities of speech, verbal quibbles, and
involved arguments—all of which obscure the
light of truth for a while! We know in part,
1 Cor 13:9 and we prophesy in part.* When the day
breathes forth life the shadows truly lie
prostrate, for when the fulness of night per-
vades all things, then no trace of shadows can
remain! For when that which is perfect is
come, that which is in part shall be done
1 Cor 13:10 away!*

III. 6. This would be enough to say about
these matters if the day had been described
as breathing and not breathing forth life, but

because of this small addition I think something more should be said to explain the shade of meaning involved. For I admit that I have long been convinced that in the sacred and precious writing [of the Scripture] there is no slightest detail which is without significance.

Aspiring is a word which we use when we desire something passionately, as for example when we say, 'He aspires to this or that honor or dignity'. By this word is signified a marvellous richness and power of the spirit, to be manifested on that day when not only our hearts but also our bodies will become spiritual* after their own fashion, and will be inebriated with the wealth of the house* of the Lord and drink of the river of his pleasures.

7. Or again, the day of righteousness has already shone* upon the holy angels, breathing upon them with continual breath and ceaseless flow the sweet mysteries of the eternal Godhead. 'The flooding river makes glad the city of God',* but that is the city of which is said 'In you is the dwelling place of all who rejoice'.* But when that day comes upon us who inhabit the earth, to breathe upon us, it will not only breathe but also breathe forth life, admitting us also into its wide embrace. Or, to go back further and give it a wider meaning, when man was fashioned from the clay of the earth, God who fashioned him, as the true account tells, breathed into him the breath of life,* and that day became for him a day of inspiration. Then, see, a baleful night, under the pretence

1 Cor 15:44

Ps 35:9

Cf. Lk 23:54

Ps 45:5

Ps 86:7

Gen 2:7

of light burst upon it; for promising an even
brighter light it quenched the new dawn with
the sudden clouds of treachery, and plunged
our first parents into terrible darkness by its
accursed counsel. Woe, woe! They did not
know, they did not understand, they walked
in the darkness in ignorance,* counting darkness as light and light as darkness.* When the
serpent offered the woman the fruit of the
tree which God had forbidden,* she ate it and
gave it to her husband. Then, as it were, a new
day began for them, for the eyes of both
were opened,* and it became for them a day
of conspiring, destroying that inspiration and
putting in its place a day of exspiring. Certainly they conspired and took counsel together against the Lord and against his Christ*
—the subtlety of the serpent and blandish-
ments of the woman, and the man's weakness. Then indeed the Lord and his Christ
spoke together: See, the man has become as
one of us,* because he has consented to the
enticements of sinners,* to the ruin of each.

8. In this day we are all born. All of us
bear branded upon us the mark of this conspiring, burnt into us; Eve still lives in our
flesh, and because of our inborn lust the
serpent schemes ceaselessly to win our consent to his rebellion. Therefore, as I said, the
saints cursed that day,* desiring that it should
be short and should quickly turn to night,*
for it is a day of discord and dispute in which
the flesh does not cease to strive against the
spirit.* The contrary law of our flesh rebels
continually against the law of the spirit.*
Thus it became a day of expiring; then, and

Ps 81:5
Is 5:20

Gen 3:6

Gen 3:7

Ps 2:2

Gen 3:22
Prov 1:10

Job 3:3, Jer 20:14
Job 3:4

Gal 5:17
Rom 7:23

ever since. 'Who is the man who will live and
not see death?'* You may call this the effect
of God's wrath, but I would rather consider it
the effect of his mercy, whereby the elect of
God, for whom all things are done, may not
long be wearied by the strife and trouble
which holds them captive to the law of sin
which is in their members.* For it is with
anguish of mind that they suffer the   shame
of their captivity and the bitterness of their
struggle.

9. Let us then make haste to respire, to
come to life out of that ancient disobedi-
ence, that conspiring, for the days of men are
brief.* May the day come and breath upon us
before we are devoured by the sighing horror
of the night and overwhelmed by the everlasting shadows of outer darkness.* Do you
wish to know where this respiration, this
coming to life, is to be found and what it
consists of? Of the spirit beginning to war
against the flesh.* You resist the flesh,† you
begin to live again; if by the spirit you begin
to mortify the works of the flesh, if you
crucify the flesh with its defects and lusts*
you live again. 'I punish my body,' says Paul,
'and bring it into subjection, so that when I
have preached to others I may not myself be
rejected'.* Those are the words of someone
who is living again—someone who has indeed
come to life. Go and do likewise,* and show
that you have come to life, and know that the
living day is breathing on you and giving
you light.

IV. Not even the night of death shall prevail

Ps 88:49

Rom 7:23

Job 14:5

Mt 8:12

*Gal 5:17
†Rom 8:13

Gal 5:24

1 Cor 9:27

Lk 10:37

against this day of new life: instead it shines in the darkness, and the darkness does not swallow it up.* Even when life departs I do not think that the light of life will fail* and I think that the saying 'Even the night about us will be light'* cannot be applied to anyone more fitly than to one who dies this way. How should he not see more clearly when he is freed from the shroud—or rather the corruption—of the body? When he is loosed from the bonds of the flesh he will surely be free among the dead,* sighted among the blind. For as in Egypt when darkness lay everywhere, the people of Israel alone in the midst of the gloom knew and saw God; for Scripture says, 'Where the people of Israel dwelt there was light',* so the just shall shine among the sons of darkness in the dreadful shadow of death* and they shall see the more clearly as they are freed from the shades of the body. But those who have not come to life again—who did not seek the light of that day or breath its air, and on whom the Sun of Righteousness did not rise*—these, I say, will go from darkness to even deeper darkness, and those who are in darkness will be in darkness still, and those who see will see more and more.

10. Here it is apposite to quote the words spoken by Our Lord, that 'to the one who has, more will be given, but as to the one who has not, even what he has will be taken away from him'.* So it is: and in death too light will be increased to those who see, and taken away from those who do not. For in proportion as these see less and less, so the others see more and more, until the horror of

Jn 1:5

Jn 8:12

Ps 138:11

Ps 87:6

Ex 10:23

1 Th 5:5, Wis 3:7

Mal 4:2

Lk 19:26

the night engulfs the first, and the life-breathing day dawns on the second; and this is the last day of both, complete blindness and perfect sight. Then nothing remains to be taken from those who are completely emptied, nor is there anything more to be given to those who are filled, unless they may expect to receive more than fulness, according to the promise made to them. Now these are the words of this promise: 'They shall put into your arms full measure pressed down and overflowing'.* You must see that anything   *Lk 6:38* which is overflowing is more than full. You will have peace of mind when you hear of this fulness and overflowing if you remember reading that God shall reign 'till eternity and beyond'.* He then will be the crown and the   *Ex 15:18* glory of that life-breathing day. That day, I say, will add its measure of fulness breathed in to the abundance of the day which breathes on them, bringing about a weight of glory* exalted above measure, so that the   *2 Cor 4:17* superabundant outpouring of light should reflect upon bodies also. For this reason it is said to be not breathing, but breathing upon   non spirans, sed them, even breathing forth life into them, and   adspirans the Holy Spirit makes this clear by the addition of the preposition *ad* because those whom he enlightens within he adorns also without, and clothes them with a robe of glory.*   *Sir 6:32*

11. And this will be reason enough to give for the meaning of the word 'aspiring', 'breathing life', and if you desire to know, the life-breathing day day is the Saviour whom we await, 'who shall change the body of our lowliness

Phil 3:20-21 to conform it to the body of his glory'.* For
he is also the one who breathes life into us
according to his operation by which he first
makes us breathe in the light which he in-
spires, so that we also will be in him a day of
respiring, of coming to life. Now our inner
2 Cor 4:16 man is renewed from day to day* and
Eph 4:23,
Col 3:10 renewed in the spirit of its mind* to be likeness of him who created it, becoming day
from the day and light from light. There are
then, two successive days in us, the one a day
of inspiration, of breathing in life, for the life
of the body, and the other a day of respiration, of coming to life, for sanctification by
grace. And there remains a life-breathing day
in the glory of the resurrection, for it is clear
that the great mystery of holiness which has
1 Tim 3:16 gone before in the head* will be accomplished
in due time in the body, and there will be
fulfilled the testimony of the prophet who
said, 'He will revive us after two days; on the
third day he will raise us up and we shall live
in his sight; we shall recognize him and we
shall follow him, that we may know him to be
Hos 6:3 the Lord!* It is he whom the angels desire to
1 Pet 1:12 look upon,* the Bridegroom of the Church,
Jesus Christ Our Lord, who is God above all
Rom 9:5 things blessed for ever.* Amen.

SERMON SEVENTY-THREE

I. WHY THE BRIDE SAYS 'RETURN'. HOW
THIS SAYING APPLIES TO THE CHURCH,
AND HOW TO THE SYNAGOGUE. II. HOW
IT APPLIES TO THE PRIMITIVE CHURCH;
WHAT IS MEANT BY A ROE AND A YOUNG
FAWN. III. WHAT IS MEANT BY THE
MOUNTAINS OF BETHEL, ON WHICH THE
BRIDEGROOM IS SOUGHT IN THE LIKE-
NESS OF A ROE OR A YOUNG FAWN.

'**R**ETURN, MY BELOVED, like a roe or a fawn.'* What? He has only just gone and yet you call him back? What has happened in so short a time? Have you forgotten anything? Yes, the Bride has forgotten everything but him, even her own self. Indeed, although she has not lost her reason, she seems now to be unsound in reason; no longer do we see that serenity she usually possesses. It is the violence of her love which brings this about. It is this which over-comes her and conquers all reserve, all consideration of fitness or caution, causing her to disregard all soberness and propriety. For see how she implores him to return, although he is only just leaving her! She even begs him to hasten, to run swiftly like a wild creature of the woods, such as a roe or a fawn. This is the

I. 1.

Sg 2:17

75

meaning of the words, and it is the portion
of the Jews.

2. Now I will examine the inner meaning,
the inspiration hidden in the deep springs of
the sacred writing, as I have received it from
the Lord.* This is my part, as I believe in
Christ. How can I extract the sweet and
wholesome spiritual feast from the barren and
tasteless letter as I do grain from the ear, a nut
from its shell, and marrow from the bone? For
the word itself I will have nothing to do
with; its taste brings the savour of the flesh,*
and to swallow it brings death, but its hidden
meaning is of the Holy Spirit.* 'The Spirit
utters mysteries,' as the Apostle declares,*
but Israel takes the veil covering the mystery
for the mystery itself.* Why is this, except
because there is a veil still over her heart?
Hers therefore is the sound of the words, but
the meaning is mine; to her the letter brings
death, to me the spirit gives life.* For it is the
spirit which gives life,* since he gives understanding; and is not understanding life? 'Give
me understanding, and I shall live',* says the
prophet to the Lord. Understanding does not
remain outside, nor does it cling to the surface,
nor run its finger over the exterior, like a
blind man, but it explores the depths and
often raises precious stores of truth, bringing
them away with great eagerness; and says to
God with the prophet, 'I will rejoice at your
words like a man who finds great treasure'.*
So indeed the kingdom of truth suffers violence, and the violent take it by storm.* The
elder brother who returned from the field* is
the type of that old earthly-minded race who

1 Cor 11:23

Job 6:6

Mt 1:20
1 Cor 14:2

2 Cor 3:15

2 Cor 3:5
Jn 6:64

Ps 118:144

Ps 118:162

Mt 11:12
Lk 15:25

are taught to labor for an earthly heritage,* *Hos 10:11*
and worn with care groan with furrowed brow
under the heavy yoke of the law, bearing the
burden and heat of the day.* He it is, I say, *Mt 20:12*
who even now stands outside because he has
no understanding,* and refuses to enter the *Cf. Eph 4:18*
house of feasting, even when invited by his
father;* so he still defrauds himself† of his **Mt 12:46-7*
share in the music and the dancing, and the *†Lk 15:28*
fatted calf. Unhappy man, refusing to find out
how good and pleasant it is for brothers to live
in unity!* This must be said to show the *Ps 132:1*
difference between the character of the
Church and of the synagogue, so the blindness
of the one may be distinguished from the
insight of the other, and the blessedness of the
one may stand in clear contrast to the unhappy foolishness of the other.

II. 3. But now let us examine the words of
the Bride, and so try to express the pure affection of her holy love that no cause of dispute
may be left in the sacred writing, nor may
there appear to be anything at all unworthy or
unseemly. If we consider the hour when the
Lord, the Bridegroom, passed from this world
to his Father,* and how this must have *Jn 13:1*
touched the heart of his household the
Church,* his newly-wedded Bride, when she *Rom 16:5*
saw herself deserted, like a widow* bereft of *1 Tim 5:5*
her only hope—I mean the Apostle who had
left everything to follow him* and had *Lk 5:11*
remained with him in his trials*—if, I say, we *Lk 22:28*
consider these things, I think we shall not find
it amazing or odd that she is so inconsolable
at his departure and so anxious for his return,

Jn 6:63

Mt 6:10

when she is thus afflicted and forsaken. In her love and her need, then, she had a twofold reason for entreating the beloved, since he could not be persuaded from leaving her and ascending where he was before,* at least to hasten to return as he had promised. When she begs and beseeches him to be like those wild beasts who have considerable speed in running, she shows how great is her soul's longing; for her no haste is sufficient. Is not this what she asks for every day, when she says in her prayer 'Thy kingdom come'*?

Lk 21:27

Phil 2:6
Is 9:6

Ps 109:5

Jm 2:13

Ps 129:3
Job 15:15
Job 4:18

Ps 31:5-6

Qo 3:14, 16, 15

Rom 3:23

4. But I think that she is pointing to the meaning of weakness no less than of speed, and of the sex of the roe and the age of the fawn. So it seems to me that she desires that even when he comes with power* to judge, he should not appear to us in the form of God* but in that form wherein he was born as a little child,* and born of a woman, one of the weaker sex. Why is this? It is that on two grounds he should be implored to be merciful to the weak in the day of wrath* and should remember on the day of judgment to put mercy before judgment.* For if he marks what is done amiss, even by the elect, who can abide it?* In his sight the stars are not clean,* and even in the angels he finds corruption.* Hear then what the elect and holy one says to God: 'You forgave the wickedness of my sin; therefore everyone who is holy shall pray to you in due time.'* Therefore even the saints have need to ask pardon for their sins,* that they may be saved by mercy, not trusting in their own righteousness. For all have sinned,* and all need mercy. It is

therefore so that he may remember mercy
when he is angry* that he is begged to appear
in the likeness of mercy; for the Apostle says
of him: 'Being found in the likeness of
a man'.*

5. And indeed it must be so. For if even
with this tempering his equity in judgment is
so great, his severity as Judge so terrible, so
lofty his majesty, so changed the appearance
of all things, that according to the prophet
the day of his coming cannot be imagined,*
what would happen if he—and it is Almighty
God I speak of—if he came as a consuming
fire,* in the power of his Godhead, in his
might and purity, like the wind teasing a leaf,
to blow away the dry stubble?* He is also
man. And the prophet says, 'Who shall look
upon him? Who shall stand at his appearing?'*
How much less could any man bear the sight
of God if he manifested himself without his
humanity, unapproachable in the brightness
of his glory, inaccessible in the loftiness of his
majesty, incomprehensible in his mighty
power? But now, when his wrath is kindled
but a little,* how graceful is the sight of his
gentle human face* to the sons of grace,
strengthening their faith, fortifying their hope,
and giving vigor to their confidence, because
his grace and mercy is with his saints,* and he
has regard for his chosen ones. Indeed God the
Father has given the power of judgement to
his Son,* not because he is his Son, but
because he is the son of man.* O truly father
of mercies! He is willing that men should be
judged by a man, so that in spite of all their
terror and apprehension of evil, his chosen

Hab 3:2

Phil 2:7

Mal 3:2

*Deut 4:24,
Heb 12:29*

Job 13:25

Mal 3:2

Ps 2:13
Dan 10:18

Wis 4:15

Jn 5:27
2 Cor 1:3

should find confidence in his humanity. Holy
David foretold this in his prayer and prophecy, saying, 'Give the king your judgements, O God', and your righteousness to
the king's son'.* So also was the promise
given by the angels when they spoke to the
apostles after the Ascension: 'This Jesus who
has been taken up from you into heaven will
come in the same manner as you have seen
him going into heaven'*—that is, in the very
form and substance of his body.

6. From all this it is clear that the Bride
has divine counsel within her, and has insight
into the mystery of the divine will, for she
proclaims in the spirit of prophecy and the
disposition of prayer that he who has chosen
a weaker nature, or rather a lower (for it will
not now be weak), shall be set on high to
judge, and shall shake heaven and earth
in his might, being girded with power against
the foolish,* but he will show himself tender
and compassionate* and altogether gentle
to his elect.* This too may be added: that to
discern one from the other he will need the
agility of the roe and the sharp sight of the
hart, and to discern in so great a confusion
and so large a crowd whom he should fix
upon and whom leap over, so that he may not
crush the righteous instead of the wicked,
when in his wrath he treads the heathen
underfoot.*

As to the wicked, there must be fulfilled
the prophecy of David, or rather the word of
God speaking by his mouth: for 'I will beat
them like dust before the face of the wind,
like mud in the streets I will destroy them.'*

Ps 71:2

Acts 1:11

Ps 64:7
Ps 85:5
Mt 24:22

Ps 55:8

Ps 17:43

Similarly another saying which he spoke by
another prophet should be recognized as fulfilled, when he returns and says to the angels,
'I have trampled them in my wrath, and trod-
den them underfoot in my displeasure.'*   *Is 63:3*

III. 7. But if anyone thinks that this should
be understood instead in the sense that
the roe should leap over the wicked and fix
upon the good, I do not dissent, as long as it is
understood that the leaps have been made to
judge between the good and the wicked. For
if I remember rightly that was what I said in a
previous discourse when the same subject was
under discussion.* But there the roe is said to   *SC 54.2-7*
leap over* according to the dispensation of   *Sg 2:8*
grace* which in this life is given to some and   *Eph 3:2, Col 1:5*
not to others, according to the just but hid-
den judgment of God; but here it refers to the
final and varying recompense of merits. And
perhaps the end of the passage, which I had
almost forgotten, may support this, for when
he says, 'Be like a roe, my beloved, and a hart
of the flock', he adds, 'on the mountains of
Bethel'.* Now in the house of God, which is   *Sg 2:17*
what Bethel means, there are no evil moun-
tains. Therefore the roe leaps on them; he
does not crush them, but makes them glad, so
that the Scripture may be fulfilled* when it   *Jn 19:36*
says, 'The mountains and hills will sing
praises before God'.* Indeed there are moun-   *Is 55:12*
tains which, according to the Gospel, may be
removed by a faith no bigger than a mustard
seed,* but these are not the mountains of   *Mt 17:19*
Bethel. For the mountains of Bethel are not
removed, but tended by faith.

Col 1:16

Mt 24:29

Ps 86:1

Heb 1:4

Ps 8:6

2 Cor 14:13

Is 53:7

Mt 26:8

1 Tim 3:16

Heb 2:9

8. If the principalities and powers,* and other companies of blessed spirits and heavenly virtues* are the mountains of Bethel, we must understand when it is said of them, 'Her foundations are in the holy hills',* that this roe is not common or to be despised, as it seemed to appear on such exalted mountains, having been made so much better than the angels and having obtained by inheritance a name which is above theirs.* Now why do we read in the Psalm that he is a little lower than the angels?* The fact that he is lower does not mean that he is not better, and the apostle and the prophet do not contradict each other, since they have received the same spirit.* For if he was made lower by condescension and not by necessity, this does not lessen his goodness but rather increases it. Indeed the prophet says that he is lower than the angels, not lesser, thus extolling his grace and removing any suggestion of injustice. His nature precludes him being less, and the cause of him being lower gives the reason for it, for he was made lower because he himself wished it;* he was made lower by his own wish and by our need. To be thus abased was to be merciful. What loss is there in this?* Indeed, what seems to detract from his majesty increases his mercy and pity. The Apostle has not passed over in silence this great mystery of his great mercy,* but says, 'We see Jesus, who for a little while was made lower than the angels, crowned with glory and honor.*

9. So much have we said with regard to the name and likeness which the Bride in her

utterance applies to the Bridegroom, without
loss to his dignity. Why do I say 'without loss
to his dignity', when not even his weakness
has remained without honor? He is a fawn, a
little child.* He is compared to a fawn,   *Is 9:6*
being born of a woman,* yet 'on the   *Gal 4:4*
mountains of Bethel',* yet exalted above the   *Sg 2:17*
heavens.* It does not say 'who exists' or 'who *Heb 7:26*
dwells' above the heavens, but 'exalted above
the heavens', so that no-one might suppose it
was said about the nature in which 'he is that
which he is'.* And when he is ranked above   *Ex 3:14*
the angels, it is not said that his life or existence is better than theirs but that he was
made* better than they. From this it would   *Heb 1:4*
appear that not only is his being from all
eternity* but that even when he was made in   *Prov 8:23*
time* he is exalted above all principalities   *Rom 1:3*
and powers,* above every creature, the first-   *Eph 1:21*
born of every creature.* So it is that 'the   *Col 1:15*
foolishness of God is wiser than men, and his
weakness stronger than men'.* The Apostle   *1 Cor 1:25*
says this, and I do not think it would be
wrong to say that this foolishness and weakness of God should be ranked before the
wisdom and power of the angels. So this passage may fitly be applied to the whole
Church.

10. Now as far as it applies as well to the
individual soul—even one soul, if it loves God
dearly, wisely, and ardently, is the Bride—each
spiritual man can ponder how this corresponds to his own experience. Yet I myself am
not afraid to speak aloud about what has been
granted me to experience. Even though it may
perhaps seem base and despicable when heard

about, this does not bother me, because no one who is spiritual will despise or misunderstand me. Yet if I hold over some part of this for another sermon, perhaps there will not be lacking those who may profit by what the Lord, in answer to my prayer, will inspire me with. For he is the Bridegroom of the Church, Jesus Christ our Lord, who is God above all, blessed for ever. Amen.*

Rom 9:5

SERMON SEVENTY-FOUR

I. HOW THIS PASSAGE APPLIES TO THE
SOUL AND TO THE WORD, AND HOW THE
COMING AND RETURNING OF THE WORD
WORKS FOR THE SOUL'S SALVATION.
II. HOW IT BEHAVES AT THE COMING
OF THE WORD, AND HOW THIS IS PER-
CEIVED. III. OF THE GRACE AND TRUTH
DEPICTED BY THE ROE AND THE YOUNG
FAWN, AND HOW GRACE IS BESTOWED
BY ITS OWN NATURE.

'**R**ETURN, she says.* Clearly he
whom she calls back is not there,
I. 1. yet he has been, not long before,
for she seems to be calling him back at the
moment of his going. So importunate a recall
shows great love on the part of the one and
great loveliness on the part of the other. Who
are these who are so taken up with charity,
these unwearying lovers, whose passion drives
them on and gives them no rest? It is my task
to fulfil my promise, and apply this passage
to the Word and to the soul,* but to do this at
all worthily I admit I need the help of the
Word himself. Certainly this topic would
more fitly be discussed by one with more
experience and awareness of this holy and
hidden love; but I cannot shirk my duty or

Sg 2:17

SC 73.10

85

disregard your requests. I am aware of the
danger, but I will not refuse to meet it, for
you force me to it.* Indeed, you force me to
walk in great matters and mysteries which
are beyond me.* Alas! how afraid I am to
hear the words, 'Why do you speak of my
delights and put my mystery into words?'*
Hear me then as a man who is afraid to speak
but cannot remain silent. My very trepidation
will perhaps justify my presumption; even
more, if it increases, your edification. Perhaps
too God will have regard to my tears. 'Return', she says. Good. He departed, he is
called back. Who will disclose to me the mystery of this change? Who will adequately explain to me the going and returning of the
Word? Surely the Bridegroom will not stoop
to inconstancy? Where can he come from?
Where can he return to, he who fills heaven
and earth?* How can he who is spirit† move
from place to place? How can any movement
of any kind be attributed to him who is God?
For he is immutable.

2. Yet let him receive this who can.* But
let us, as we proceed with caution* and
singleness of purpose* in our exposition of
this sacred and mystical utterance,* follow
the example of Scripture, which speaks of the
wisdom hidden in the mystery,* but does so in
words familiar to us, & which, even as it enlightens our human minds, roots our affections on
God, and imparts to us the incomprehensible
and invisible things of God* by means of
figures drawn from the likeness of things
familiar to us, like precious draughts in vessels
of cheap earthenware.*

2 Cor 12:22

Ps 130:1

Cf. Ps 49:16

*Jer 23:24
†Jn 4:24

Mt 19:12
Eph 5:15
Prov 11:20
Is 3:3

1 Cor 2:7

Rom 1:20

Cf. 2 Cor 4:7

Let us then follow this discourse of pure
love,* and say that the Word of God, God   *Ps 11:7*
himself, the Bridegroom of the soul, comes
to the soul and leaves it again as he wishes,*   *1 Cor 12:11*
but we must realize that this happens as a
result of soul's sensitivity, and is not due to
any movement of the Word. Indeed, when the
soul is aware of the influence of grace she
acknowledges the presence of the Word; but
when she is not, she mourns his absence, and
again seeks his presence, saying with the
prophet, 'My face has sought you; your face,
Lord, I will seek.'* How could she do other-   *Ps 26:8*
wise? For when so sweet a bridegroom with-
draws from her she cannot desire any other,
nor even think of another. It must be that
when he is absent she seeks him ardently, and
when he goes away she calls him back. Thus
the Word is recalled—recalled by the longing
of the soul* who has once enjoyed his sweet-   *Is 26:8*
ness. Is longing not a voice? It is indeed, and a
very powerful one. Then the Psalmist says,
'The Lord has heard the longing of the
poor'.* When the Word departs therefore, the   *Ps 9:38*
one unceasing cry of the soul, its one unceasing desire, is 'return'—until he comes.*   *1 Cor 11:26*

3. Now show me a soul which the bridegroom, the Word, is accustomed to visit
often, whom friendship has made bold, who
hungers for what it has once tasted, whom
contempt of all things has given leisure, and
without hesitation I will assign it the voice
and name of the Bride, and will consider the
passage we are studying applicable to it. So
indeed is the speaker portrayed. For when she
calls him back she proves that she deserves

his presence, even if not in its fulness. Otherwise she would have called to him to come,
not to return. But the word 'return' signifies a
recalling. Perhaps it was for this very reason
that he withdrew, that the more eagerly she
recalls him, the more closely she will cleave to
him. For he once pretended that he was
going further, not because that was his intention, but because he wanted to hear the words,
Lk 24:28-9   'Stay with us, for evening is coming on'.*
And another time, when the apostles were in
a boat pulling on the oars, he walked on the
Mk 6:48   sea,* making as though he would pass them
by, not because he intended to, but to try
their faith and draw out their prayers. Then,
so the Evangelist says, they were troubled and
Mk 6:49   cried out, thinking that he was a ghost.*
This kind of pious pretence, this saving gift,
dispensed by the Word when in the body does
not lose its effect when the Word in spirit
employs it in his own spiritual manner in dealing with a soul devoted to him. He makes to
go past, desiring to be held back, and seems to
go away, wishing to be recalled; for he, the
Word, is not irrevocable; he comes and goes
according to his own good pleasure, visiting
Job 7:18   the soul at daybreak* and then suddenly
putting it to the test. His going is part of his
own purpose, and his return is always part of
his own will; both are within his infinite
wisdom. His reasons he alone knows.

4. Now it is clear that his comings and
goings are the fluctuations in the soul of
which he speaks when he says, 'I go away,
Jn 14:28   and come again to you',* and, 'a little while
and you shall not see me, and again a little

while and you shall see me.'* Oh little while, *Jn 16:17*
little while! How long a little while! Dear
Lord, you say it is for a little while that we do
not see you. The word of my Lord may not
be doubted, but it is a long while, far too
long. Yet both are true: it is a little while
compared to what we deserve, but a long
while to what we desire. You have each
meaning expressed by the prophet Habak-
kuk: 'If he delays, wait for him, for he will
come, and will not delay.'* How is it that he *Hab 2:3*
will not delay if he does delay, unless it is
that he comes sooner than we deserve but not
as soon as we desire? For the loving soul is
carried away by her prayers and drawn on by
her longing; she forgets her deserts, closes her
eyes to the majesty of the Bridegroom but
opens them to the pleasure he brings, looking
only at his saving grace,* and in that putting *Ps 11:6*
her confidence. Then without fear or dread
she calls back the Word, and confidently asks
again for his delights, calling him, with
accustomed familiarity, not 'Lord' but 'beloved': 'Return, my beloved'.* And she adds *Sg 2:17*
'Be like a fawn or a doe on the mountains
of Bethel'. But more of this later.

II. 5. Now bear with my foolishness for a
little.* I want to tell you of my own experi- *2 Cor 11:1*
ence, as I promised. Not that it is of any
importance.* But I make this disclosure only *2 Cor 12:1*
to help you, and if you derive any profit from
it I shall be consoled for my foolishness; if
not, my foolishness will be revealed. I admit
that the Word has also come to me—I speak
as a fool*—and has come many times. But *2 Cor 11:17*

although he has come to me, I have never
been conscious of the moment of his coming.
I perceived his presence, I remembered afterwards that he had been with me; sometimes
I had a presentiment that he would come, but
I was never conscious of his coming or his
going.* And where he comes from when he
visits my soul, and where he goes, and by
what means he enters and goes out, I admit
that I do not know even now; as John says:
'You do not know where he comes from or
where he goes.'* There is nothing strange in
this, for of him was it said, 'Your footsteps
will not be known'.* The coming of the Word
was not perceptible to my eyes, for he has no
color; nor to my ears, for there was no sound;
nor yet to my nostrils, for he mingles with the
mind, not the air; he has not acted upon the
air, but created it. His coming was not tasted
by the mouth, for there was no eating or drink-
ing, nor could he be known by the sense of
touch, for he is not tangible. How then did he
enter? Perhaps he did not enter because he
does not come from outside? He is not one of
the things which exist outside us.* Yet he does
not come from within me, for he is good,* & I
know that there is no good in me. I have ascended to the highest in me, and look! the
word is towering above that. In my curiosity I
have descended to explore my lowest depths,
yet I found him even deeper. If I looked outside myself, I saw him stretching beyond the
furthest I could see; & if I looked within, he
was yet further within. Then I knew the truth
of what I had read, 'In him we live & move &
have our being'.* And blessed is the man in

Ps 120:8

Jn 3:8

Ps 76:20

1 Cor 5:12
Ps 51:11

Acts 17:28

whom he has his being, who lives for him and
is moved by him. ‖

6. You ask then how I knew he was pres-
ent, when his ways can in no way be traced?*   *Rom 11:33*
He is life and power,* and as soon as he en-   *Heb 4:12*
ters in, he awakens my slumbering soul; he
stirs and soothes and pierces my heart,*   *Sg 4:9*
for before it was hard as stone,* and diseased. *Si 3:27, Ez 11:19,
So he has begun to pluck out and destroy, to   36:26*
build up and to plant, to water dry places and
illuminate dark ones;* to open what was   *Cf. Jer 1:10*
closed and to warm what was cold; to make
the crooked straight and the rough places
smooth,* so that my soul may bless the   *Is 40:4*
Lord, and all that is within me may praise
his holy name.* So when the Bridegroom,   *Ps 102:1*
the Word, came to me, he never made known
his coming by any signs, not by sight, not by
sound, not by touch. It was not by any
movement of his that I recognized his coming; it was not by any of my senses that I perceived he had penetrated to the depths of my
being. Only by the movement of my heart, as
I have told you, did I perceive his presence;
and I knew the power of his might* because   *Eph 1:13*
my faults were put to flight and my human
yearnings brought into subjection. I have
marvelled at the depth of his wisdom* when   *Qo 7:25*
my secret faults* have been revealed and   *Ps 18:13*
made visible; at the very slightest amendment
of my way of life I have experienced his goodness and mercy; in the renewal and remaking
of the spirit of my mind,* that is of my in-   *Eph 4:23*
most being, I have perceived the excellence of
his glorious beauty,* and when I contemplate   *Ps 49:2*
all these things I am filled with awe

Ps 150:2

and wonder at his manifold greatness.*

7. But when the Word has left me, all these spiritual powers become weak and faint and begin to grow cold, as though you had removed the fire from under a boiling pot, and this is the sign of his going. Then my soul

Mt 26:38,
Ps 41:6, 12;
Ps 42:5

must needs be sorrowful* until he returns, and my heart again kindles within

†Ps 108:22

me†—the sign of his returning. When I have had such experience of the Word, is it any wonder that I take to myself the words of the Bride, calling him back when he has withdrawn? For although my fervor is not as strong as hers, yet I am transported by a desire like hers. As long as I live the word 'return', the word of recall for the recall of Word, will be on my lips.

As often as he slips away from me, so often shall I call him back. From the burning desire of my heart I will not cease to call

Ps 20:3

him, begging him to return,* as if after some-

Jdg 18:23

one who is departing,* and I will implore him

Ps 50:14

to give back to me the joy of his salvation,* and restore himself to me.

III. I assure you, my sons, I find joy in nothing else if he is not here, who alone gives me joy. And I implore him not to come

Is 55:11

empty-handed* but full of grace and

Jn 1:14

truth,* as is his nature—as he did yesterday

Gen 31:5

and the day before.* Herein is shown his like-

Sg 2:17

ness to a roe or a fawn,* for his truth has the sharp eyes of a roe, and his grace the gladness of a fawn.

8. I need both of these: I need truth that I may not be able to hide from him, and grace

that I may not wish to hide. Indeed, without
both of these his visitation would not be
complete, for the stark reality of truth would
be intolerable without grace, and the gladness
of grace might appear intolerable without
truth. Truth is bitter unless seasoned with
grace, and devotion without the restraining
power of truth can be capricious and uncon-
trolled and even arrogant. Have many have
received grace without profit because they
have not also accepted a tempering measure
of truth? In consequence they have luxuriated
in it too much,* without reverence or regard   *Is 42:1*
for truth; they have not considered the ripe
maturity of the roe, but have given themselves
over to the caprices and gladness of the fawn.
Thus it has come about that they have been
deprived of the grace which they wished to
enjoy by itself. To them it could be said,
though too late, 'Go then, and learn what it
means* to serve the Lord in fear, and rejoice   *Mt 9:13*
in him with awe.* The holy soul which had   *Ps 2:11*
said in her abundance 'I shall never be
moved',* and then feels that the Word has   *Ps 29:7-8*
turned his face away finds herself not only
moved but much troubled; thus she learns in
sorrow that with the gift of devotion she
needed also the steadying power of truth.
The fulness of grace, then, does not consist of
grace alone. What use is it to know what you
ought to do, if you are not given the will to
do it? But what is the use of having the will if
you have not the power? How many have I
known who are the sadder for knowing the
truth because they could not plead ignorance
as an excuse when they knew the demands

of truth but did not fulfil them?

9. Neither then is sufficient without the other. That is an understatement: neither has any value without the other. How do we know this? Scripture says, 'If a man knows what is good, and does not do it, that for him is sin';* and again, 'If a servant knows the will of his master and does not perform it duly, he shall be severely beaten'.* This refers to truth. What is said of grace? It is written, 'And after the sop Satan entered into him.'* It is speaking of Judas, who received the gift of grace, but because he did not walk in truth with the Lord of truth,* with truth as his teacher, he gave place in himself to the devil.* Hear again, 'He fed them with the finest wheat, and with honey from the rock he satisfied them.'* Who are they? 'The enemies of the Lord have lied to him.'* Those whom he has fed with honey and wheat have lied to him and become his enemies, because they did not add truth to grace. In another place it says of them, 'The strange children have lied to me, the strange children have grown weak and are limping off their paths.'* How can they help limping when they are supported on the one foot of grace, and do not stand on truth? Their fate will last for ever, like that of their prince,* who himself did not stand on the truth, but was a liar from the beginning,* and therefore heard the words 'You have destroyed your wisdom through your own splendor.'* I do not desire a splendor which can rob me of wisdom.

10. Do you ask what this elegance is, so harmful and so dangerous? It is your own.

Jm 4:17

Lk 12:47

Jn 13:27

2 Jn 4

Eph 4:27

Ps 80:17
Ps 80:16

Ps 17:46

Ps 80:16

Jn 8:44

Ez 28:17

Do you still not understand?* I will speak more plainly. It is a splendor which is inward-looking and personal. It is not the gift we condemn, but the use made of it. For, if you notice, Satan is said to have lost his wisdom not because of splendor but because of his own elegance. Surely the splendor of an angel and the splendor of a soul are one and the same. What is an angel or a soul without wisdom but a rough, shapeless mass? But with wisdom there is a splendor not only of form but of beauty.* But Satan lost this when he appropriated it as his own, so that to lose wisdom through his own elegance to lose it through his own wisdom. Possessiveness brings about the loss. It was because he was wise in his own eyes,* not giving God the glory,† nor returning grace for grace,* and not walking in grace following truth† but distorting it for his own purposes, that he lost it. Indeed, to possess it is to lose it. If Abraham, as the Apostle says, was justified by his works, he possessed something in which to glory, but not before God.* 'I am not safe,' I would say. 'Anything I do not possess before God I have lost.' Nothing can be as lost as that which is outside the presence of God. What is death but the loss of life? Perdition is nothing but alienation from God. 'Woe to you who are wise in your own eyes, and prudent in your own minds.'* It is said of you, 'I will destroy the wisdom of the wise & frustrate the prudence of the prudent.'* They have lost wisdom, because their own wisdom has caused them to be lost. How can they not lose everything, who are themselves lost; and those whom God does not re-

Mt 15:16

Cf. Wis 10:1
formatus . . .
formosus

*Prov 26:5
†Jn 9:24
*Jn 1:16
†2 Jn 4

Rom 4:2

Is 5:21

1 Cor 1:19

Mt 12:12
Mt 25:2

Rom 1:22
Mt 25:12

Mt 7:23

Jn 1:17
Rev 3:20

Ps 142:2

Jn 15:26
Ps 85:5

Lam 3:25
Rom 9:5

cognize are indeed lost.*

11. Now the foolish virgins*—whom I do not think to have been foolish in other respects than by believing themselves wise they became silly*—they, I tell you, will hear God saying, 'I do not know you'.* So those who have made use of grace to perform miracles to enhance their own reputation will likewise hear the same condemnation, 'I do not know you'.* From this it is quite clear that grace brings no profit where there is no truth in one's intention, but rather brings harm. Both [grace and truth] are found in the Bridegroom's presence. 'Grace and truth came by Jesus Christ,' says John the Baptist.* If then the Lord Jesus knocks at my door,* with one of these gifts and not the other— and he is the word of God, the Bridegroom of the soul—he will enter not as a bridegroom but as a judge. God forbid that this may ever happen! 'Enter not into judgement with your servant.'* May he enter as one who brings peace, joy, and gladness; but may he also enter with the gravity of maturity, to purify my joy and control my arrogance with the stern gaze of truth. May he come as a leaping fawn and a sharp-eyed roe, to pass over my offences and look at them only with pity and forgiveness. May he come down as from the mountains of Bethel, full of joy and radiance, descending from the Father,* sweet and gentle,* not scorning to become and to be known as the Bridegroom of the soul who seeks him,* for he is God, blessed above all for ever.* Amen.

SERMON SEVENTY-FIVE

I. OF THE MEANING OF THE SAYING
'I SOUGHT HIM ON MY BED' ETC., AND
WHY HIS FINDING IS UNNOTICED.
II. THREE REASONS WHY THOSE WHO
SEEK ARE DISAPPOINTED: TIME, LUKE-
WARMNESS, AND PLACE. III. HOW IN
THIS PASSAGE THE REASON FOR DIS-
APPOINTMENT IS PLACE. IV. THE MEAN-
ING OF 'WHOM MY SOUL LOVES', AND
WHAT THE NIGHTS ARE THROUGH WHICH
THE BRIDE SOUGHT THE BRIDEGROOM.

'IN MY BED night after night I sought
him whom my soul loves'.* The
I. 1. Bridegroom has not returned when
the Bride calls him back with cries and
prayers. Why not? He wishes to increase her
desire, test her affection, and exercise her
faculty of love. He is not displeased with her,
he is concealing his love. But he has been
sought for, and we must ask whether he may
be found, for he did not come when he was
called. Yet the Lord said, 'Everyone who
looks finds';* and the words used to recall
him were 'Return, my beloved, like a roe or a
fawn'.* When he did not return at this call,
for the reasons I have given, then she who
loved him became more eager and devoted

Sg 3:1

Mt 7:8

Sg 2:17

herself eagerly and entirely to seeking him.
First she sought him in her bed, but she found
him not at all. Then she arose and wan-
dered through the city, going to and fro
among the streets and squares,* but she did
not meet him or catch sight of him.* She
questions everyone she meets, but there is no
news; nor is this search and this disappointment confined to one night or one street,
for she says, 'I sought him night after night'.*
How great must be her longing and her ardor,
that she does not blush to rise in the night
and be seen running through the city, ques-
tioning everyone openly about her beloved,
not to be deflected for any reason from her
search for him, undaunted by any obstacle,
undeterred by any desire for rest, or by a
bride's modesty, or by terrors of the night!*
Yet in all this she is still disappointed of her
hope.* Why? What is the reason for this long,
unrelenting disappointment, which induces
weariness, foments suspicion, inflames impa-
tience, acts as a stepmother to love and a
mother to despair? If he is still concealing his
love, it is too painful.

2. Perhaps this concealment may have
had some good purpose for a time, until
everything was concentrated on calling him,
or recalling him. But now she is seeking him
and calling for him; what then can be the
purpose of any further concealment? If these
are incidents in a human marriage, and the
love spoken of is physical love, as a superficial reading might imply, then I must leave
the matter to those it concerns;* but if my
task is to give an answer which will satisfy, as

Sg 3:1-2
Sg 3:3

Sg 3:1

Ps 90:5

Ps 77:30

Acts 18:15

far as I can, the minds and affections of those who seek the Lord, then I must draw from Holy Scripture—in which they trust that life to be found*—something of vital spiritual importance, that the poor may eat and be satisfied and their hearts may live.* And wherein is the life of their hearts but in Jesus my Lord, of whom one who lived in him said, 'When Christ our life shall appear, you also will appear with him in glory.'*? Let him come into our midst so that it may be truly said to us, 'One stands among you whom you do not know.'*

I do not know how the Bridegroom, who is Spirit, can fail to be recognized by spiritual men, who have made sufficient progress in the spirit to say with the prophet, 'The Lord's Anointed is the spirit of life to us',* and with the Apostle, 'If we think of Christ in a worldly way, we do not know him.'* Is it not he whom the Bride was seeking? Truly he is the Bridegroom, both loving and lovable. Truly, I tell you, he is the Bridegroom, and his flesh is truly food and his blood truly drink;* he is wholly and truly himself, since he is none other than truth itself.*

3. Why then is this Bridegroom not found when he is sought, when he is looked for so anxiously and so untiringly, now in the bed of the Bride,* now in the city, or even in the streets and squares? For he himself says, 'Seek and you shall find',* and, 'He who seeks finds',* and the prophet says, 'How good you are, Lord, to the soul who seeks you',* and again, holy Isaiah says 'Seek the Lord while he may be found'.* How then shall the

Jn 5:39

Ps 21:27

Col 3:4

Jn 1:26

Jeremiah, Lam 4:20

2 Cor 5:16

Jn 6:56

Jn 14:6

Sg 3:1-2

Mt 7:7

Mt 7:8

Lam 3:25

Is 55:6

Mt 26:54

Scriptures be fulfilled?* For she who is here said to seek him is not one of those to whom he said 'You will seek me and you will not find me'.*

Jn 7:34

II. But notice three reasons which occur to me why those who seek are disappointed: perhaps they seek at the wrong time, or in the wrong way, or in the wrong place. For if any time were the right time to seek, why does the prophet say, as I have already mentioned, 'Seek the Lord while he may be found'?* There must be a time when he will not be found. Then he adds that he should be called upon while he is near,* for there will be a time when he will not be near. Who will not seek him then? 'To me', he says, 'every knee shall bow'.* Yet he will not be found by the wicked; the avenging angels will restrain them and prevent them from seeing the glory of God.* In vain will the foolish virgins cry,* for the door is shut and he will certainly not go out to them. Let them apply to themselves the saying 'You will seek me and you will not find me'.*

Is 55:6

Ibid.

Is 45:24

Cf. Jn 11:40
Mt 25:10

Jn 7:34

4. But now is the acceptable time, now is the day of salvation.* It is clearly the time for seeking and for calling, for often his presence is sensed before he is called. Now hear his promise: 'Before you call me', he says, 'I will answer. See, I am here.'* The psalmist, too, plainly describes the generosity of the Bridegroom, and the urgency: 'The Lord hears the crying of the poor; his ear hears the movement of their hearts.'* If God is to be sought through good works, then while we have time

2 Cor 6:2

Is 65:24

Ps 9:38

let us do good to all men,* all the more   *Gal 6:10*
because the Lord says clearly that the night is
coming when no-one can work.* Will you   *Jn 9:4*
find any other time in ages to come* to seek   *Heb 6:5*
for God, or to do good,* except that time   *Eph 4:28*
which God has ordained, when he will remem-
ber you?* Thus today is the day of   *Job 14:13*
salvation,* because God our king before all   *2 Cor 6:12*
ages has been working salvation in the midst
of the earth.*   *Ps 73:12*

5. Go then, wait in the midst of hell for
the salvation which has already been worked
in the midst of the earth. What use to dream
of obtaining pardon among the everlasting
fires,* when the time for mercy has already   *Is 33:14*
passed?* No victim will be left to atone for   *Ps 101:14*
your sins,* you will be dead in your sins.†   *Heb 10:26
The son of God is not crucified again.*   †Jn 8:24
He died once, he dies no more.† His blood,   *Heb 6:6
which was poured out over the earth,* does   †Rom 6:10, 9
not go down to hell. All the sinners on earth   Mt 23:35*
will drink of it,* but it is not for demons to   *Ps 74:9*
claim for putting out their flames, nor for
men who have allied themselves with demons. It was his soul, not his blood, which
once descended there; and this was the
portion of the spirits in prison.* That was his   *1 Pet 3:19*
one visit there, by which he was present in
spirit, while his body hung lifeless on earth.
His blood bedewed and watered the thirsty
earth; his blood refreshed it;* his blood   *Ps 64:10*
brought peace to these in heaven and those
on earth,*but to those in hell he did not bring *Eph 1:10*
peace. His soul did descend there that once,
as I said, and wrought redemption* in part;   *Lk 1:68*
not even at that moment would he cease

2 Cor 6:2

Mt 7:8

Cf. Rom 10:20

Ps 31:6

his works of mercy, but beyond that he will add nothing. Now is the acceptable time,* now is the right time to seek him, when he who seeks will find,* if he seeks at the right time and in the right way. This is one reason which prevents the Bridegroom from being found by those who seek him,* that they do not seek him at the right time.* But this is not what hinders the Bride, for she calls upon him and seeks him at the right time. Nor is she lukewarm, negligent, or perfunctory in her search, but ardent and untiring, as she should be.

Sg 3:1

III. 6. There remains the third reason which we must consider, whether she is looking in the wrong place. 'In my little bed night after night I sought him whom my soul loves.'* Perhaps he should not be sought in a little bed, but in a bed, since the whole world is too narrow for him? Still, I am not displeased at the 'little bed', for I know that Our Lord became little; 'He was born for us as a little child.'* Rejoice and sing praises, O dweller in Zion, for great is the Holy One of Israel among you.* That same Lord who is great in Zion* is little and weak among us,* and needs to lie down, and to lie in a little bed. Was his tomb not a little bed? Was the manger not a little bed? Was the Virgin's womb not a little bed? It was not a little bed but a great bed, of which the Father spoke when he said to the Son, 'Out of the womb of the morning have I begotten you'.* That womb cannot be thought of as a bed at all; it is a place from which to rule rather than

Is 9:6

Is 12:6

Ps 98:2

Cf. Is 53:10;
1 Cor 1:25

Ps 109:3

in which to rest. For he abides in the Father
and with the Father he rules all things; our
sure belief is that he does not lie down but
sits at the right hand of God the Father.* He
himself says that the heavens are his throne,†
not his bed; in his own place, that is in the
heavens, he does not seek comfort in weakness, but holds the emblems of power.

The Apostles'
Creed
†Cf. Is 66:1

7. Rightly then does the Bride say, '*my
little bed*', for any weakness in God* is clearly
not part of his nature, but of ours. It was
from us that he took all those things which
he took upon himself for our sake: his birth,
his being nursed, his death and burial. The
mortality of the new-born babe is mine,
the weakness of the child is mine, the death
on the cross is mine, and the sleep in the
tomb is mine. All these are the former
things which have passed away, and behold,
all things are made new.* 'In my little bed I
sought him whom my soul loves.'* What?
Were you seeking him in your bed, when he
had already returned to his own? Did you
not see the Son of Man ascending where he
was before?* He has now changed the stable
and the tomb for heaven, and are you still
looking for him in your little bed? He is not
here, he is risen.* Why do you seek the strong
in a cot, the great in a bed, the glorified in a
stable? He has entered into the Lord's
powers,* he has clothed himself in majesty
and strength;* and look, he who lay under
the grave-stone sits above the Cherubim.* He
lies down no more, he is enthroned; and are
you preparing comforts for him as though he
were reclining? To speak with greater accu-

1 Cor 1:25

*2 Cor 5:17; Rev
21:4–5.*
Sg 3:1.

Jn 6:63

Mk 16:6

Ps 70:16
Ps 92:1
Ps 98:1

racy, he is either enthroned as judge or stands as advocate.

8. For whom then do you keep watch, O holy women? For whom do you buy spices and prepare ointments?* If you knew the greatness of this man whom you are going to anoint, how, though dead, he is free from the dead,* I think you would beg instead to be anointed by him.* Is it not he whom God has anointed with the oil of gladness above his fellows?* How happy you will be† if you can return in exultation and say, 'of his fulness we have all received'?* For it was like this.† The women who had gone to anoint him returned themselves anointed. How could they not, when they were anointed with the joy of the news of his fragrant resurrection? 'How beautiful are the feet of those who spread the good tidings of peace.'* Sent by the angel they did the work of an evangelist,* and became the apostles of the apostles, and while they hastened in the early morning to give their news of the mercy of God,* they said, 'We will run in the fragrance of your perfumes'.* Since that day, then, the Bridegroom has been sought in vain in a little bed, for until then the Church had known him according to the flesh, that is, according to the flesh, that is, according to the weakness of the flesh,* but she knows it no more. True, Peter and John sought him later in the sepulchre,* but they did not find him. Do you see how fitly and appropriately each of them could then say, 'In my little bed I sought him whom my soul loves; I sought him but I did not find him'?* For his flesh, which

Lk 23:56

Ps 87:6
Jn 4:10

*Ps 44:8
†Lk 6:22

*Jn 1:16
†Gen 1:7

Rom 10:15
Mt 28:7

Ps 91:3

Sg 1:3

2 Cor 5:16;
Rom 6:19

Jn 20:3

Sg 3:1

was not of the Father,* rid itself of every
infirmity by the glory of resurrection before
it went to the Father. It girded itself with
strength,* it put on light as a garment,† that
it might present itself to the Father in the
splendor and beauty which was its own.

Jn 14:28

Ps 64:7
†*Ps 103:2*

IV. 9. How beautifully then does the bride
speak when she says not 'him whom I love',
but 'him whom my soul loves'. For the love
by which one loves spiritually', whether its
object is God, or an angel, or another soul, is
truly and properly an attribute of the soul
alone. Of this kind also is the love of justice,*
truth, goodness, wisdom, and the other virtues. But when a soul loves—or rather yearns
for—anything of a material nature* be it
food, clothing, property, or anything else of a
physical or earthly nature, that love is said to
pertain to the flesh rather than to the soul. So
when the Bride says that her soul loves her
Bridegroom, she uses an unusual expression,
but one which is none the less appropriate,
for it shows that the Bridegroom is a spirit,
and that he is loved with a spiritual, not a
physical, love. She is right, too, when she says
that she sought him night after night. For if,
as Paul says, 'Those who sleep sleep at night,
and those who are drunk are drunk at night',*
I think that it is not absurd to say that those
who are ignorant are ignorant at night, and
likewise those who seek seek at night. For
who would seek what he obviously possesses?*
Now the day shows openly what the night
concealed, so that in the daytime you may
find what you sought by night. It is night,

Ps 44:8

Rom 8:5

1 Thess 5:7

Rom 10:20

then, while the Bridegroom is being sought,
for if it were day, he would be seen among

2 Thess 2:7   us,* and would not be sought at all. Enough
about that subject, except that, as the Bride
said, not 'by night' but 'night after night',
some questions may arise about the significance of there being more than one night.

10. If you have no better explanation, I
suggest this as a possibility. This world has its
nights—not few in number. I say the world
has its nights, but it is almost all night, and
always plunged in complete darkness. The
faithlessness of the Jews, the ignorance of
pagans, the perversity of heretics, even the

carnalis   shameless and degraded behavior* of Catho-
animalisque   lics—these are all nights. For surely it is night
conversatio   when the things which belong to the Spirit of
1 Cor 2:14   God are not perceived?* There are as many
nights as there are sects among heretics and
schismatics. In those nights you will look in
vain for the sun of justice and the light of
truth, that is, the Bridegroom, because light

2 Cor 6:14   has nothing to do with darkness.* 'But', you
say, 'the Bride would not be so blind or so

Jn 1:5   foolish as to look for light in darkness,* or to
search for the beloved among those who do
not know him or love him.' But she does not
say that she is seeking him now night after
night, and cannot find him. No, what she says
is, 'Night after night I sought him whom my
soul loves'. Her meaning is that when she was
a child she understood like a child and thought

1 Cor 13:11   like a child,* looking for truth where it was
Dan 7:16   not, wandering but not finding it,† as it says
†Mt 18:12; Lk 11:24 in the psalm, 'I have strayed like a 'lost

sheep'.* Indeed she mentions that she was   *Ps 118:176*
still in a little bed, being as it were tender in
age and young in sensitivity.

11. If, when you read 'In my little bed
I sought him whom my soul loves', you
understand that she was reclining, then the
meaning is not 'I sought him in my little
bed', but 'when I was in my little bed I
sought him'; that is to say, when I was young
and weak,* and quite unfit to follow the   *Rom 5:6*
Bridegroom wherever he went,* to the steep   *Rev 14:4*
and lofty heights of his glory, I encountered
many who, knowing my desire, said to me,
'Look, here is Christ; look, there he is'.* But   *Mk 13:21*
he was not here nor was he there. Yet by
encountering these men I became wiser,* for   *Ps 21:3*
the nearer I came to them and the more
carefully I questioned them, the sooner I saw
that the truth was not in them,* and the surer   *Jn 8:32*
I became of it. I sought him and did not find
him, and I perceived that what was masque-
rading as day was in fact night.

12. And I said, 'I will arise and go about
the city; through the streets and squares will I
seek him whom my soul loves'.* Notice now   *Sg 3:2*
that when she says 'I will arise' she is lying
down. Quite rightly. How could she not arise
when she heard of the resurrection of her
beloved? Yet, O blessed one, if you are risen
with Christ, set your heart on the things which
are above, not on those below; you must seek
Christ above, where he sits on the right hand
of the Father.* But you say, 'I will go about   *Col 3:1-2*
the city'.* For what purpose? 'The wicked   *Sg 3:2*
prowl on every side.'* Leave that to the Jews,   *Ps 11:9*
of whom the prophet rightly prophesied:

'They shall suffer hunger like dogs, and go
about the city.'* And another prophet says,
'If you enter the city, behold those who are
sick with hunger',* which would not be so if
the bread of life* were to be found there.
He has arisen from the heart of the earth, but
did not remain on earth. He has ascended to
where he was before. He who came down is
indeed he who has ascended,* the living bread
which came down from heaven,* he who is
the Bridegroom of the Church, Jesus Christ
Our Lord, who is God above all, blessed for
ever.* Amen.

Ps 58:7

Jer 13:18
Jn 6:35; Mt 12:40

Eph 4:10
Jn 6:41

Rom 9:5

SERMON SEVENTY-SIX

I. HOW THE BRIDE SOUGHT THE BRIDE-
GROOM THROUGH THE STREETS AND
SQUARES, AND WHY THIS WAS IN VAIN,
SINCE HE HAD ASCENDED TO HEAVEN.
II. OF THE FATHER GLORIFYING THE
SON AND THE SON THE FATHER.
III. HOW FAITH FINDS WHAT INTELLECT
FAILS TO FIND, AND OF THOSE WHO
GUARD THE CITY OF GOD, WHICH IS AT
ONCE THE BRIDE AND THE FLOCK.
IV. THE GUARDING OF THE CITY, THE
ADORNING OF THE BRIDE, AND THE
PASTURING OF THE SHEEP, AND WHAT
SORT OF MAN SHOULD BE CHOSEN FOR
THIS TASK.

I. 1. 'THROUGH THE STREETS and squares I will seek him whom my soul loves.'* She still has the understanding of a child,* and, I suppose, she imagines that when he had come forth from the tomb he would appear openly and continue to teach the people* and heal the sick* as before, and reveal his glory in Israel,* so that those who promised to accept him if he came down from the cross* might perhaps do so when he rose from the dead. But he had finished the work which the Father had given him to do,* and the Bride

Sg 3:2
1 Cor 13:11

Lk 5:3
Lk 9:2
Jn 2:11
Mt 27:42

Jn 17:4

should have understood this from the cry which he uttered on the cross when he was

Jn 19:30

at the point of death: 'It is finished'.* He had no need to put himself again at the mercy of the people, who would not be likely to believe in him even then. He was returning with haste to his Father, who would say to him, 'Sit at my right hand until I set your enemies beneath your feet'.* For being now

Ps 109:1

lifted up above the earth he would draw all

Jn 12:32

men to him* with the greater strength of divine power. But she, desiring to enjoy him, yet not understanding the mystery, thought that he should be sought through the streets and squares. So she is again disappointed in her search and says, 'I sought him but did not

*Sg 3:2
†Jn 18:9

find him',* so fulfilling the words† he spoke, 'Because I go to the Father, and you shall see

Jn 16:16

me no more'.*

2. But perhaps she will say, 'How then will

Rom 10:14

they believe in one whom they do not see?'* —as though faith depends on sight and does

Rom 10:17

not rather come by hearing.* Is there any difficulty in believing what one sees? Is there any merit in trusting the evidence of one's eyes? But if we hope for what we do not see, we wait in patience,* and patience brings

Rom 8:25

merit. 'Blessed are they who have not seen,

Jn 20:29

yet have believed.'* So, giving room for virtue, he withdraws himself from her sight, that she may not be robbed of the merit of faith. Moreover, it is now time for him to return to his own place. 'What is his own place?' you ask. It is at the right hand of the Father. For he did not think it robbery to be equal with

Phil 2:6

God, since he is in the form of God.* Let the

place of the only-begotten Son be where all
outrage and malice is banished and is no more
seen. Let his seat then be beside his Father,*   *Jn 5:23*
not below, so that all men may honor the
Son as he honors the Father; thus it shall be
seen that he is equal to the Father in majesty;
he will not be considered inferior or sub-
ordinate. But in the meantime the Bride has
no such thoughts, but runs hither and thither,
as though besotted with love, seeking with
her eyes for him who can now be discerned
not by sight, but by faith. She does not think
that Christ should enter into his glory* before   *Lk 24:26*
the glory of his resurrection is known through-
out the world, so that all wickedness may be
checked, the righteous rejoice, the disciples
exult, and the heathen be converted. And
when the truth of his words has been clearly
shown by this risen presence, he will be
glorified by all. You are wrong, O Bride.
These things must indeed be done,* but in   *Mt 24:6*
their own time.

3. But meantime, consider whether it may
not be more worthy of and more fitting to
supreme righteousness not to give what is
holy to the dogs, or to cast pearls before
swine;* whether perhaps in accordance with   *Mt 7:6*
the Scriptures the wicked man should be
removed, lest he look upon the glory of
God;* or whether faith should be dis-   *Is 26:10*
appointed, since it is more clearly proved in
believing what is not seen*—and thus what is   *Jn 20:29*
hidden from the unworthy may be reserved
for those who are worthy of it, so that those
who are filthy may be filthy still, and the
righteous may become more righteous,* if   *Rev 22:11*

Ps 118:28
they do not grow weary and fall asleep.*
Let the heavens and the heaven of heavens
*Is 34:4
†Ps 118:116
decay* and be disappointed of their hope,† as
long as the Almighty Father himself is not
Ps 77:30
thwarted of his heart's desire,* and the only-
begotten Son is not any longer hindered from
entering into his glory—which would be most
unsuitable! What glory do you imagine can
be given by mortals which would be worthy
to keep him even for a moment from the glory
which had been prepared for him by his
Father from all eternity?

II.   Remember, too, that it is quite wrong for
the fulfilment of the Son's petition to be
deferred any longer. What petition do I
mean, you ask. The one, of course, which
Jn 17:1
says, 'Father, glorify the Son'.* No, I think
that this petition was made as a prophecy
rather than as a prayer, for what is asked
for without reservation is within the power of
taking of him who asks. So the Son's petition
is a matter of divine economy rather than
necessity, for whatever he receives from the
Father he also gives with the Father.

4.   It must also be said that not only does
the Father glorify the Son, but the Son also
glorifies the Father. Let no-one say that the
Son is inferior to the Father because he is
glorified by the Father, for he himself glorifies the Father. Notice, he says, 'Father,
glorify your Son, that your Son may glorify
Ibid.
you'.* Perhaps you still think that the Son
should be considered inferior, because to
receive glory from the Father in order to give
it back to the Father implies a lack of glory.

But it is not so. Hear what he says: 'Father,
glorify me with the glory which I had with
you before the world was made.'* *Jn 17:5*
If the Son's
glory is not inferior or secondary, since it has
been for all eternity, then the Father and the
Son give equal glory to each other; and if this
is so, in what does the primacy of the Father
consist? For where there is co-eternity there
is surely equality, and the equality is such
that the glory of both is one, since they are
themselves one.* *Jn 17:22*
It seems to me, then, that
when he says on another occasion, 'Father,
glorify your name',* *Jn 12:28*
he asks nothing other
than to be glorified himself; and he receives
from his Father the reply, 'I have glorified it,
and will glorify it again'.* *Ibid.*
This reply in itself
gives no small glory to the Son. And he was
given greater glory and higher honor at the
fords of the Jordan by the testimony of
John: his marking out by the dove,* *Jn 1:32*
and the
voice saying, 'This is my beloved Son'.* *Mt 3:17*
But
greatest majesty and glory was that which
attended him on the mountain in the company of the three disciples,* *Mt 17:1-5*
both by that
same voice sounding* again from the hea- *2 Pet 1:17*
vens, and by the remarkable beauty and
wonder of his physical transfiguration, and
again by the witness of the two prophets who
also appeared there and talked with him.

5. It remains then for him to be glorified
once more, in accordance with his Father's
promise, and that will be the fullness of
glory, to which nothing can be added. But
where will this blessing be given? Not, as she
supposed, in the streets and squares,* *Lk 14:21*
unless
it be in those of which it is said, 'Your streets,

O Jerusalem, shall be paved with pure gold,
Tob 13:22   and alleluia shall be sung in your by-ways'.*
There, indeed, he has received from his
Father that glory whose like cannot be found
Cf. 2 Chron 6:14   even in the heavens.* For to which of the
Heb 1:5, 13   angels was it said, 'Sit at my right hand'?*
Indeed, none of the angels is found fit to
assume the greatness of this glory, nor any
among the other higher orders of the blessed.
To none of them has come that proclamation
of singular glory, to none of them has it
been given to experience in himself its work-
ings. Thrones, Dominations, Principalities and
Col 1:16   Powers* certainly desire to look upon him in
Cf. 1 Pet 1:12   his glory,* but none presume to compare
Ps 109:1   themselves with him. So it is to 'My Lord'*
that the proclamation was made, to him
alone that it was granted by the Lord to sit
at the right hand of his glory, for he alone is
co-equal in glory, consubstantial in being,
identical by generation, alike in majesty, and
co-eval in eternity. There, there it is that he
Mt 7:8   who seeks will find him* and will see his
glory—not glory as of one among many, but
Jn 1:14   glory as of the only-begotten of the Father.*

III. 6. What then, O Bride, will you do? Do
you think you can follow him there? Dare
you, can you penetrate to that holy hiding
place, that hidden sanctuary, to look upon
the Son in the Father and the Father in the
Son? Assuredly not. Where he is, you cannot
Jn 13:36   come now, but you shall come hereafter.*
Come then, follow, seek him; do not let that
1 Tim 6:10   unapproachable brightness and glory* hold
you back from seeking him or make you

despair of finding him. 'If you can believe, all
things are possible to him who believes.'* 'The   *Mk 9:22*
Word is near you, in your mouth and in your
heart.'* Believe, and you have found him.   *Rom 10:8*
Believing is having found. The faithful know
that Christ dwells in their hearts by faith.*   *Eph 3:17*
What could be nearer? Therefore seek him
confidently, seek him faithfully. 'The Lord is
good to the soul who seeks him.'* Seek him   *Lam 3:25*
in your prayers, follow him in your actions,
find him in faith. How can faith fail to find
him? It reaches what is unreachable, makes
known what is unknown, grasps what cannot
be measured, plumbs the uttermost depths,
and in a way encompasses even eternity itself
in its wide embrace. I speak in faith [when I
say that] I believe the eternal and blessed
Trinity, although I do not understand it, and
I hold fast by faith what I cannot grasp with
my mind.

7. But someone says, 'how shall she be-
lieve without a preacher,* since faith comes   *Rom 10:14*
by hearing,* and hearing comes by the word   *Rom 10:17*
of a preacher? God will provide for this.*   *Cf. Gen 22:8*
Look, they are here already, they who are to
instruct the new bride in the things she needs
to know, and prepare her for her marriage to
the heavenly Bridegroom,* and to teach her   *Rev 21:2*
the faith and counsel her in the ways of
holiness and true religion. For hear what she
says next. 'The watchmen who guard the city
have found me.'* Who are these watchmen?   *Sg 3:3*
Surely those of whom the Saviour said in the
Gospel, 'Blessed are they whom the Lord
finds watching when he comes.'* How good   *Lk 12:37*
they are, these watchmen who keep watch

while we sleep, as though they would answer
for our souls!* How good they are, these
guardians who are watchful in spirit and spend
the night in prayer,* who scout the snares of
the enemy, forestall the plots of the wicked,*
detect their traps, avoid their entanglements,
tear their nets, and frustrate their evil designs!
These are lovers of their brethren* and the
christian people, who pray a lot for their
people and for all the Holy City. These are
they who care with all their heart for the
Lord's flocks committed to their charge, and
early in the morning call upon the Lord*
who made them and pray to the Lord most
high. They watch and pray, for they know
that of themselves they cannot keep the
city safe, for 'unless the Lord keep the city,
the guard keeps watch in vain.'*

8. Now since the Lord commands us to
'Watch and pray, so that you do not enter
into temptation',* it is clear that without
this twofold activity of the faithful, and the
constant care of those who guard them,
neither the city nor the Bride nor the sheep
can abide in safety. Do you ask what difference there is between these three? They
are one and the same. The city, because an
assembly of souls; the Bride, because beloved;
sheep because gentle. Do you want to know
why the Bride is called a city? St John says, 'I
saw the Holy City, the New Jerusalem, coming down from God out of heaven, prepared
as a bride adorned for her husband.'* This
and [the figure] of the sheep will become
clear to you and full of meaning if you
remember how the Lord in his wisdom

Margin references:

Heb 13:17

Lk 6:12
Ps 82:4, 25:5

2 Macc 15:14

Si 39:6

Ps 126:1

Mt 26:41

Rev 21:2

entrusted the sheep to the first shepherd—
I mean St Peter—and urged him with such
persistence to tend it lovingly.* He would not
have taken such care over this unless he had,
from the depth of his conscience acknowl-
edged himself as the Bridegroom. Listen to
this, you friends of the Bridegroom,* if
friends you are. But to call you friends is not
enough; those who are granted the privilege of
such great intimacy should rather be called
close and dear friends. It was not pointlessly
that Our Lord, in handing over the sheep,
said three times, 'Peter, do you love me?'* It
was, I think, as though Jesus had said: 'Unless
your conscience bears witness that you love*
me and love me so strongly and completely—
more than you love your possessions, your
family, and even yourself—that this threefold
command of mine is fulfilled, you must not,
on any account, take this charge upon you,
nor must you have any dealings with these
sheep of mine for whom my blood was shed.'
A speech to inspire dread, and to strike terror
into the heart of any tyrant, however bold.

9. Therefore give heed, you who have
been chosen for this ministry;* give heed, I
say, to yourselves and to the precious charge
which has been entrusted to you. It is a city:
watch then, and keep it in peace and safety.
It is a bride: see to her adornment. It is sheep:
see that they are pastured. These three considerations may well have a bearing on Our
Lord's threefold inquiry.

IV. Again, the care of the city must be
threefold if it is to be effective; it must be

Jn 21:15-17

Jn 3:29

Jn 21:17

Rom 9:1

*Eph 4:12;
Acts 1:17*

protected from violence of tyrants, from the snares of heretics, and from temptations of evil spirits. The Bride must be adorned with the threefold adornments of good works, good character, and good disposition. Likewise the sheep must all be pastured on the Scriptures, which are the Lord's legacy,* but there are differences among them. There are commandments, the rough pasturage appointed for the stubborn and unspiritual as a guide to life and discipline,* and there is the lush grass of dispensations granted out of pity to the weak and timid; and there is the strong solid grass of the counsels provided for the healthy, whose faculties have been trained to distinguish between good and evil.* The young, the lambs, then, must be given the milk of exhortation to drink, not solid food.* Therefore good and faithful shepherds never cease to feed their flock with good and choice examples—from their own lives rather than from other people's. If they offer those of other people and not their own, this is to their discredit, and their flock will not profit. I, for example, apparently carry the responsibility of being your shepherd. Now if I hold up to you as examples the compassion of Moses, the patience of Job, the mercy of Samuel, the holiness of David, and so on, but if I myself remain without compassion, impatient, unmerciful, and anything but holy, my exhortations would, I fear, be unpalatable and you would not be keen to listen. I can only leave this to the goodness of God, that he may supply what is lacking in me and correct my mistakes. The good shepherd will

Si 24:11

Si 45:6

Heb 5:14

1 Cor 3:2

also take care to have salt in himself, the salt
of which the Gospel speaks,* for he knows
that a discourse seasoned with salt* is both
pleasing to the taste and profitable to salvation. This is all I have to say for the moment
about guarding the city, adorning the bride,
and feeding the sheep.

10. But I want to speak a little more fully
about these things for the benefit of those
who, in their immoderate desire for honors,
rashly take upon themselves burdens too
heavy for them, and expose themselves to
danger. I want them to know what it is they
are coming for; as the Scriptures say: 'Friend,
why have you come here?'* If I am not
mistaken, a man needs to be strong, spiritual,
and loyal merely to guard the city; he must be
strong to repulse the attacks of enemies,
spiritual to detect their ambushes,* and loyal
so that he may not serve his own interests.
And it is quite undeniable that for the train-
ing and direction of souls, which is what is
meant by the adorning of the Bride, there
must be a considerable measure of discipline
and great diligence. Everyone, therefore, who
is called to this work, must burn with the same
zeal as that conspicuous lover of the Lord's
Bride who said, 'I am jealous for you with a
godly jealousy, for I betrothed you to one
husband to present you as a chaste virgin to
Christ'.* Then, how can an ignorant shepherd
lead the Lord's flock into the pastures of the
oracles of God? And if he has learning without goodness it is to be feared that he would
not so much nourish them with the richness of
his teaching as harm them with the barrenness

Mk 9:49

Col 4:6

Mt 26:50

1 Cor 13:5

2 Cor 11:2

of his life. Therefore it is sheer temerity for
anyone to undertake this task unless he has
the necessary knowledge and lives an exem-
plary life. But see, I must make an end—
though this is not the end of what I have to
say. I am summoned to attend to another
matter, and one which is of lesser importance. I am torn in pieces,* and I do not
know which is harder to bear, to be dragged
away from the one or pulled to the other.
But I suppose it would be even worse to
suffer both together. O the bondage of
necessity! What I do is not what I choose,
but what I detest.* But take note where I have
left off, so that we may take it up again
quickly as soon as we are free to do so, in the
name of the Bridegroom of the Church, Jesus
Christ Our Lord, who is God above all,
blessed for ever. Amen.*

Dan 13:22

Rom 7:19

Rom 9:5

SERMON SEVENTY-SEVEN

I. A DENUNCIATION OF UNWORTHY
SHEPHERDS. II. THE KIND OF SHEP-
HERDS BY WHICH THE BRIDE SAYS SHE
WAS FOUND, AND THE LOVE OF TRUTH
WHICH SHE HAS LEARNED FROM THEM.
III. OF THOSE WHO PRESUME TO SET
THEIR OWN WAY OF LIVING WITHOUT A
GUIDE, AND HOW THE BRIDE SAYS SHE
WAS FOUND.

I. 1. 'NOW WE ARE FREE to continue. Yesterday we described the kind of guides we should choose to have on the path we travel.* However, we find that the guides we have are not of this kind, but very different. Not all those whom you see today waiting on the Bride and hanging around her, as the expression is, are friends of the bridegroom.* There are very few of them among all her lovers* who are not concerned with their own interests.* It is gifts that they love; they cannot love Christ as well, for they have given their allegiance to Mammon.* See how they go about, dressed elegantly and fashionably in bright colors,* like a bride coming out of her chamber.* If you saw one of them in the distance, you would think it was the Bride rather than an attendant. Where do you suppose they get

Ps 141:4

Jn 3:29
Lam 1:2
1 Cor 13:5

Cf. Mt 6:24
Ps 44:15
Ps 18:6

121

Gen 24:53

Ps 73:21

*1 Cor 9:7
†Jn 10:10

Ps 13:4

Ps 78:7
Hos 4:8

Is 61:2

this wealth from, these splendid clothes and rich foods, and all these vessels of gold and silver,* if it is not from the Bride? So it comes about that she is left poor, naked, and in want,* her appearance piteous, unkempt, bruised, and weak. Now this is not to adorn the Bride but to despoil her; not to guard her but to destroy her. It is not to defend her but to expose her to danger; not to provide for her but to prostitute her. It is not to feed the flock,* but to butcher and devour it.† The Lord says of these, 'They eat up my people as though they were bread',*and, 'They have devoured Jacob and laid waste his dwelling-place.'* And in another place the prophet says, 'They eat up the sins of my people',* as if to say, 'They demand a price for sins, but do not bother to care for sinners as they should.' Can you mention anyone in authority who is not more concerned with emptying people's purses than rooting out their vices? Where is the man who turns away anger by his prayer, and preaches the acceptable year of the Lord?* But we are speaking of comparatively trivial matters; heavier judgment waits for more important ones.

2. It is pointless to spend time on such as these, for they do not listen to us. If what we say is written down, they scorn to read them or, if they do happen to read them, they launch a diatribe against me, although they might more properly direct it against themselves. Let us then leave these, for they do not find the Bride, but sell her, and let us consider those who the bride says have found her, those whose office and ministry the others

we mentioned have inherited,* but not their
zeal. Everyone wants to be their successors,
but few their imitators. Would that they were
found as meticulous in discharging their
duties as they are eager in running after their
dignities! Then they would watch over* and
take care of* the bride who has been found
and entrusted to their care. Indeed, they
would watch over themselves, and not allow
it to be said of them, 'My lovers and kinsmen
approached and stood aloof from me'.* This
complaint is altogether just, and it cannot be
applied to any age more justly than to ours.
For not content with not watching over us,
our guardians do us actual harm, being sunk
in so deep a sleep that they do not wake at
the thunder of divine wrath, and therefore do
not tremble at their own peril. So it is that
they care neither for themselves nor for their
people, and they perish with those they
destroy.

II. 3.   But who are those watchmen by whom
the bride says that she has been found?
Indeed they are apostles, apostolic men.
These are the ones who guard the city, that is
the church which they have found, and they
watch over her the more diligently when they
see her in danger from evil which attacks her
from within her own household. It is written,
'a man's enemies are those within his own
household'.* For they who have defended her
with their own blood* will surely not leave
her without their protection, but will guard
her and keep her safe by day and night,* in
life and in death. And if 'in the sight of the

Acts 1:17

Mt 24:43
Eph 4:3

Ps 37:12

Mic 7:6
Heb 12:4

Jdth 7:4

Ps 115:15
Lord the death of his saints is precious,* I
have no doubt that they exercise their guar-
dianship as much more powerfully in their
deaths, as their authority is greatly streng-

Ps 138:17
thened by it.*

4. But you may say, 'You speak as though
you have seen these things with your own
eyes; but such things are hidden from human
view'. I would answer: 'You trust the witness
of your own eyes; the witness of God is

1 Jn 5:9
greater.* For he says, "I have set watchmen
upon your walls, O Jerusalem. They shall

Ps 62:6
never be silent by day or night".'* 'But', you
say, 'that referred to the angels.' 'I do not

Heb 1:14
deny it; "they are all ministering spirits".'*
But who shall say that I should not include
with them those who are equal in authority to
the angels themselves, but are perhaps nearer
to us in affection and compassion, since they
have greater kinship with us? Also, they have
endured the same sufferings and miseries as

2 Cor 1:6
we now endure for a time.* Will these holy
souls therefore not be filled with greater care
and pity because they must remember ex-
periencing the same troubles? Is it not their
voice which says 'we have passed through fire
and water, and you have brought us into a

Ps 65:12
place of refreshment'?* Would they leave us
in the midst of the flames and great waters
which they have passed through, without
taking the trouble to stretch out a hand to
us, their children? Surely not.' It is well with
you, mother Church, it is well with you in

Ps 118:54
this place of pilgrimage:* help comes to you

Ps 123:8
from heaven and earth.* Your guardians do

Ps 120:4
not slumber or sleep.* Your guardians are the

holy angels, your watchmen are the spirits
and souls of the righteous.* Anyone is correct in feeling that you have been found by
both alike, and by both alike you are guarded.
And they each have their special care for
you: the saints because they will not themselves be made perfect without you; the
angels because without you their full number cannot be restored, for, as you all know,
when Satan and his myrmidons fell from
heaven,* the number of the heavenly host was
greatly diminished. Thus all things await their
consummation from you, some the comple-
tion of their numbers, others the fulfilment
of their desires. Be sure then that it is your
voice which says in the Psalm, 'The just wait
for me, until you reward me'.*

5. Notice now that it is not said that she
has found them, but rather that she has been
found by them—and that, I suspect, is because
they have been called for this very purpose.
'How shall they preach unless they are sent?'*
And there is a saying in the gospels: 'Lo, I
send you forth,'* and, 'Go, preach the gospel
to every creature'.* And so it was; she sought
the bridegroom, and this was not hidden from
him, for he himself had urged her on to seek
him, and given her the desire to fulfil his
commands* and follow his way of life.† But
there must be someone to instruct her and
teach her the way of prudence.* Therefore
he sent out, as it were, gardeners to cultivate
and water his garden,† to train and strengthen
her in all truth, that is, to teach her and give
her sure tidings of her beloved, since he is
himself the truth which she seeks and which

Dan 3:86

Lk 10:18

Ps 141:8

Rom 10:15

Lk 10:3
Mk 16:15

*1 Kgs 3:12
†Si 45:6

*Is 40:14 = Magni-
ficat antiphon of
17 December
†Cf. 1 Cor 3:6

her soul truly loves. Indeed, who is the
faithful and true lover of the soul if not he
through whom the truth is loved? I am endowed with reason; I am capable of receiving
truth, but this would be vain if I lacked
the love of truth. He is the fruit of this vine,

Cf. Rev 22:16   and I am the root.* I am not safe from the
axe if I am found apart from him. It is
doubtless by nature's endowment that the

Gen 1:26   divine likeness shines forth,* and in this I am
superior to all living creatures. Therefore my
soul ventures to respond to the chaste embraces of truth, and so to rest in the complete
assurance of his love and sweetness, provided

Gen 18:3   that it finds favor in the eyes* of so great a
bridegroom, and that he accounts it worthy
to attain to his glory, and even presents it
to himself as a bride without spot or wrinkle

Eph 5:27   or anything of that kind.* What judgement,
what penalty do you suppose a man will
deserve if he shows indifference to so great a
gift of God? But we will speak of this
another time.

III. 6. But now the Bride does not find him
whom she sought, but is found by those whom
she did not seek. Let this be a warning to
those who are not afraid to enter the paths

Ps 15:11   of life* without anyone to guide and teach
them, but act as their own pupils as well as
their own teachers in the spiritual life. Nor
are they satisfied with this; they even collect

2 Tm 4:3   disciples, the blind leading the blind.† How
†Mt 15:14   many have we seen wander from the right
path, to their great peril, as a result of this?
For their ignorance of the wiles and tricks of

Satan brings it about that those who began in
the spirit finish in the flesh.* They are led
seriously astray and fall damnably. Such men
should see that they walk carefully* and take
warning from the Bride, who could not reach
her beloved until she was met by those whose
ministry she used to gain knowledge of her
beloved, to learn the fear of the Lord.*
Anyone who pretends to give his confidence
to his director will find he is giving it to a
seducer. The man who sends his sheep to
pasture without a guardian is a shepherd not
of sheep but of wolves.*

7. Now let us turn to the Bride and hear
what she means when she says she was
found. The word seems to me to be used in a
rather unusual sense. She speaks as though the
Church had come from one place, whereas,
according to the word of the Lord, it came
from the east and from the west,* and from
all the ends of the earth.* But it has never
at any time been gathered together in one
place* where it could be found by the
apostles or the angels, to be led or directed
to him whom its soul loves.* Was it found
before it was gathered together? It was not,
for it did not exist. Therefore if she had said
that it was gathered together, or had met, or
(a term more applicable to the Church) been
called together by those who preach the
Gospel, I should have simply passed it by
without any comment. For they are fellow-
workers with God,* and are heard to say, 'He
who does not gather with me scatters.'* I
should not think it strange if anyone said that
it was founded or built up by them, for they

Gal 3:3

Eph 5:15

Ps 33:12

Jn 10:12

Mt 8:11
Mt 12:42

Cf. Jn 11:52

Sg 1:6

1 Cor 3:9
Lk 11:23

Mt 16:18
Mt 7:25

acted in union with him who says in the Gospels, 'Upon this rock I will build my church',* and, 'It was founded upon a rock'.* But now she says none of these things, but makes the strange claim that she was found, and she causes us to hesitate a while, suspecting some hidden meaning which we ought to examine more carefully.

8. I would have preferred, I admit, to continue without engaging in an examination which I do not feel up to. But when I remember in how many obscure and difficult matters I have been conscious of support beyond my expectation, when you were lifting up your hearts to God, I am ashamed of my lack of faith. And suppressing my apprehension I take up the task which in my diffidence I had shunned. The help to which I am accustomed will, I hope, be at hand; if not, what I intend to say will not be idle when I have such friendly hearers. But this will form the beginning of my next sermon, for we must bring this one to a close. May he who is the Bridegroom of the Church grant that you may not only remember what you have heard, but take it to heart with love and effectually put it into practice—he who is Jesus Christ our

Rom 9:5

Lord, God above all, blessed for ever.* Amen.

SERMON SEVENTY-EIGHT

I. HOW GOOD, THE ANGELIC HOST, AND MAN WORK TOGETHER FOR THE WELL-BEING OF THE BRIDE. II. OF THREE INSTANCES WHEN GOD ACTS FIRST: PREDESTINATION, CREATION, AND INSPIRATION; AND WHY THE BRIDE COULD NOT BE FOUND FROM THE BEGINNING, BUT ONLY AFTER INSPIRATION. III. HOW SHE IS RIGHTLY CALLED BRIDE, BEING PREPARED BY GOD, AND AFTER HER PREPARATION FOUND BY THE WATCHMEN.

I. 1. WE STOPPED, if I remember right, at the consideration of the word 'found', hearing, with some reservations, that the Bride stated she had been found by the watchmen. Also we gave the reasons for our reservations and caution, and decided to discuss the question a little. But we could not undertake this when we were approaching the end of the sermon.* ^{in calce sermonis} Now therefore we must complete what we began. In treating of this great mystery,* ^{Eph 5:32} which the teacher of the Gentiles* inter- ^{1 Tim 2:7} preted as the holy and chaste union of Christ and his Church, the very work of our salvation, I find three agents cooperating together: God, an angel, and man. Surely God cannot

129

but be actively concerned in the nuptials of his beloved Son? He must be, with his whole will. He could indeed accomplish it of himself, without any other help; but they without him can do nothing.* When he gave them a part in this ministry,* therefore, it was not for his sake but for theirs. For he has set merit for men through work as he said, 'The laborer is worthy of his hire',* and, 'Every man shall receive his reward according to his own labor',* whether he plants or waters what has been planted.* When he uses the ministry of angels for the salvation of the human race, is it not so that the angels may be loved by men? For it is clear that men are loved by the angels because they are not unaware that the losses in their ranks will be made up by men. Indeed, it would not be right that the kingdom of charity, which men and angels are to rule together, should be governed by other laws than those of mutual love and pure affection for each other and for God.

2. There is, however, a great difference in the ways in which these agents work, for each plays his part according to his dignity. God accomplishes what he wills by the simple act of willing, without irresolution, without change, free from considerations of time and place, motives or persons. For he is the Lord of hosts, who judges all things in tranquillity.* He is Wisdom, graciously ordering all things.* The angels likewise work without irresolution, but they are not free from variations of time and place. But man, for his part, is subject both to mental irresolution and to mental and physical change. He is

Jn 15:5
Eph 4:12

Lk 10:7

Cf. 1 Cor 3:8
1 Cor 3:7

Jer 11:20 &
Wis 12:18

*Wis 8:1 = Magnificat antiphon for 17 December

bidden to work out his salvation with fear and trembling,* and to eat his bread in the sweat of his brow.†

II. 3. After that explanation, I should like you to consider with me three elements in the glorious work of our salvation which God, its Author, reserves to himself, and in which he forestalls all his helpers and fellow-workers: predestination, creation, and inspiration. Of these, predestination had its beginning not with the birth of the Church, not even with the beginning of the world; it was before all time. Then creation came into being with time, and inspiration within time, where and when God wills. In accordance with predestination there was never a time when the Church of the Elect was not before God's face. If the unbeliever wonders at this, let him hear something even more wonderful: there was never a time when she was not loved and delighted in.* Why should I not proclaim boldly the mystery in the heart of God, made known to me by one who could reveal heavenly designs. I mean Paul, who did not scruple to divulge this hidden saying as he did many others which came to him from the riches of divine goodness.* 'He has blessed us', he said, 'with every spiritual blessing in Christ in the heavenly kingdom; in Christ he chose us before the foundation of the world, that we should be holy and without blemish in his sight in love'; and he added, 'he has predestined us to be his adopted sons through Jesus Christ, according to his pleasure, to the praise of the glory of his grace, which he has

numquam non dilecta

Rom 2:4

Eph 1:3-6

bestowed upon us in his beloved Son.'* And there is no doubt that these words are spoken with the voice of all the elect—they are the Church. But who, even among the blessed spirits, would ever have been able to find the Church, hidden in the deep womb of eternity, unless God, to whom eternity belongs, had chosen to reveal it?*

Mt 11:27

4. But when, at the Creator's bidding, the Church appeared and was seen in visible and material form, she was not immediately perceived by any angels or men, because she was not recognized, being overshadowed by the earthly appearance of men,* and covered with the shadow of death.* But none of the sons of men have entered this life without the veil of disorder, except he who came without sin,* Emmanuel,† who although he was one of us and for our sakes put on the garment of our curse* and the likeness of our sins, yet had no share in its reality. For you must know that he appeared in the likeness of sinful flesh that by sin he might condemn sin in the flesh.* Apart from him, all men have come into the world in the same condition,* whether they are elect or wicked. There is no distinction;* all have sinned,† and all bear the badge of their shame. Therefore even if the Church had already been created and had its being among created things, she could not have been found or recognized by any creature, but in a strange manner lay hidden for a time, both in the bosom of predestination and in the accursed lump of our pitiable condition.*

1 Cor 15:49

Job 10:21

*Ps 14:2
†Is 7:14

Ps 108:18 &
Gal 3:13

Cf. Rom 8:3

Wis 7:6

*Rom 10:12
†Rom 3:23

*Cf. William of
St Thierry,
Mirror of Faith
5 (CF 15:13);
Augustine,
De correptione
et gratia
I.10.26
(PL 44:932).

5. But the Church, who was concealed

from all eternity by the wisdom of predestination, and had not been fully revealed by the power of creation, was in due course manifested in visible form by grace, working in the way I have described before as inspiration. It was breathed into the human spirit by the Bridegroom, for the preparation of the gospel of peace,* that is, to prepare the way† for the Lord and for the Gospel of his glory* in the hearts of all who have been predestined for life. Now the watchmen would have labored in vain* in their preaching if they had not been forestalled by grace. But when they saw the word running swiftly,* the people of all nations turning readily to the Lord, all tribes and tongues united in the faith,* and all the ends of the earth* gathered into the one mother, the Church, they recognized the riches of grace* which had been kept hidden in the secret of eternal predestination* and rejoiced to have found her whom the Lord had chosen for his Bride before time began.

*Eph 6:15
†Mal 3:1, Lk 1:17
*2 Cor 4:4

Ps 126:1

Ps 147:15

Cf. Rev 5:9
Ps 2:8

Eph 1:7

Cf. Col 1:26

6. It is clearly not without significance, I think, that the Bride says she was found by them, for she recognizes that she was gathered in by them, not chosen; they found her, they did not convert her.

III. The conversion of anyone must be ascribed alone to him to whom all men must say, in the words of the Psalm, 'Convert us, O God our salvation'.* But I cannot apply to them as fitly the term 'finding' as 'conversion'. It would be truer to say that the Lord does not find a soul so much as forestall it

Ps 84:5

and make a way for it.* Forestalling renders finding unnecessary. What need has he to find anything when there is nothing he has not always known? It has been said, 'The Lord knows those who are his'.* And what does he say himself? 'I know whom I have chosen from the beginning.'* Clearly he has foreknown from all eternity him whom he has chosen, loved and established, and we cannot rightly say that she was found by him. I think one may truthfully say that he prepared her to be found by him. We have the record of a witness and we know that his record is true.* 'I, John, saw the holy city, the new Jerusalem, coming down from the hand of God in heaven, like a bride adorned for her husband.'* This is the record of one of the watchmen, one of those who guard the city.* Now hear the words of him who prepared her, pointing her out as it were with his finger to the watchmen, but using another metaphor: 'Lift up your eyes and look on the fields; they are already white'*—that is, ready for harvesting. When the head of the household knows that everything is ready, he summons his laborers to work,* so that without great labor on their part they can exult and say, 'We are fellow-workers with God'.* What is left for them to do? Only to look for the Bride, and when they have found her, to give her tidings of her beloved. They are friends of the Bridegroom.* Therefore it is the Bridegroom's glory, not their own, which they seek. And they will not have a heavy task, for she is here, and already seeks him with her whole heart, because her will has been made ready by the Lord.

7. Now although they have not yet spoken to her, she asks them about her beloved, and she who has herself been forestalled forestalls her guides, and says, 'Have you seen him whom my soul loves?'* She was right to say that she had been found by those who guard the city, for she knew that she had been already known and forestalled by the Lord of the city. This was not their action; they found her so. It was thus that Cornelius was found by Peter,* and Paul by Ananias.† Both had been forestalled and prepared by the Lord. Who could have been more fully prepared than Saul, who he cried out with heart and voice, 'Lord, what do you want me to do?'* So also Cornelius who, through the almsgiving and prayers which God inspired, was found worthy to come to the faith.* Thus also Philip found Nathanael,* but the Lord had already seen him under the fig-tree. That was surely his preparation. In the same way Andrew is said to have found his brother Simon,* but the Lord had seen him before, and had known that he would be called Cephas, the man with faith like a rock.*

8. We read also that Mary was found with child by the Holy Spirit.* I think that the Lord's Bride is like his Mother in this. For if she had not been found filled with the Holy Spirit, she would not have questioned in so familiar a fashion those who found her, asking them about him in whom the Spirit has his being. But she, speaking out of the fulness of her heart,* said, 'Have you seen him whom my soul loves?'* She knew how

Sg 3:3

Acts 10:1
†*Acts 9:10*

Acts 9:6

Acts 10:3-4
Jn 1:45-8

Jn 1:41-2

1 Pet 5:9

Mt 1:18

Mt 12:34
Sg 3:3

Lk 10:23-4

blessed are those who have seen him,* and she asked them wonderingly, 'Are you those to whom it has been granted to see him whom kings and prophets desired in vain to see? Are you they who were found worthy to see wisdom in the flesh, truth in bodily form, God in man? Men say, 'Here he is', or 'there

Lk 17:21

he is',* but I think it safer to put my trust in you who ate and drank with him after he

Acts 10:41

arose from the dead.'*

I think enough has been said of the Bride's question to the watchmen. If not, I will say more in another sermon. But it must have been made quite clear that the Bride, the Church, was forestalled by the Holy Spirit

1 Cor 2:7,
Rom 8:29

and predestined by God before all ages,* and that he prepared her for his beloved son to be

Is 26:4
Eph 5:27
Is 35:1-2
Rom 15:6

an everlasting joy throughout all ages,* holy and without blemish in his sight,* growing like a lily and blossoming for ever* before the Lord, the father of my Lord Jesus Christ,* the Bridegroom of the Church, he who is

Rom 9:5

God, blessed above all for ever.* Amen.

SERMON SEVENTY-NINE

I. WHY THE BRIDE ASKS 'HAVE YOU
SEEN HIM WHOM MY SOUL LOVES?', AND
WHAT IT MEANS WHEN SHE LEAVES THE
WATCHMEN BEHIND. II. OF THE BOND
OF LOVE BY WHICH THE BRIDE HOLDS
THE BRIDEGROOM AND WILL NOT LET
HIM GO, AND WHY SHE PREPARES TO
LEAD HIM TO HER MOTHER'S CHAMBER.

'**H**AVE YOU SEEN HIM whom
my soul loves?'* O strong and   *Sg 3:3*
I. 1. burning love, O love urgent and
impetuous, which does not allow me to think
of anything but you, you reject all else, you
spurn all else but yourself, you are contented
only with yourself! You throw order into
confusion, ignore moderation; you laugh* at   *Col 2:15*
all considerations of fitness, reason, modesty
and prudence, and tread them underfoot.*   *2 Cor 10:5*
All the Bride's thoughts and words are full of
nothing but your music and fragrance, so
completely have you taken possession of
her heart and tongue. 'Have you seen him
whom my soul loves?' she asks—as though
they would know what she meant. Who is it
whom your soul loves, for whom you en-
quire? Has he no name? Who are you and
who is he? I speak like this because of the
strange manner of speech and extraordinary

137

disregard for names, quite different from the rest of the Scriptures. But in this marriage-song it is not the words which are to be pondered, but the affections behind them. Why is this, except because the sacred love which is the subject of the whole canticle cannot be described in the words of any language, but are expressed in deed and truth?* And love speaks everywhere; if anyone desires to grasp these writings, let him love. It is vain for anyone who does not love to listen to this song of love, or to read it, for a cold heart cannot catch fire from its eloquence.* The man who does not know Greek cannot understand Greek, nor can anyone without Latin understand someone speaking Latin, and so on. So, too, the language of love will be meaningless jangle to one who does not love, like sounding brass or tinkling cymbal.* But as they— I mean the watchmen—have received from the Spirit* the desire to love, they know what the Spirit says, and as they understand the expressions of love, they are ready to reply in similar terms, that is, in loving zeal and works of mercy.

2. Indeed they instruct her so well about the one for whom she inquires that she can say, 'I had left them behind a little while when I found him whom my soul loves.'* She is right to say 'a little while', for they gave her a brief word;* in fact, they gave her the creed. It was indeed necessary that as she passed by she should meet those from whom she was to learn the truth, yet she had to leave them behind. If she had not, she would not have found the one she sought. You can have no

1 Jn 3:18

Ps 118:140

1 Cor 13:1

Jn 7:39

Sg 3:4

verbum abbreviatum:
Cf. Rom 9:28

doubt that they urged her to do so. For they did not preach themselves, but the Lord Jesus,* who is without question above them and beyond them. It is for this reason that he says, 'Come to me, all who desire me'.* But it was not enough for her to meet them as she passed by; she was told to pass on and leave them behind,* for he whom she was searching for had also passed on. He passed not only from death to life,* but passed on to glory. How should she not also pass on? She could not come to him otherwise than by following in the footsteps where he had gone.*

2 Cor 4:5

Si 24:26

to pass by =
transire; to pass
on = pertransire.
*Jn 5:24

Rev 14:4

3. If I may make my meaning clearer, if my Lord Jesus had indeed risen from the dead but had not ascended into heaven, one could only say that he had passed by, not that he had passed on to glory, and that the Bride who seeks him must also only pass by, and not pass on. But since he had passed by in his Resurrection and had passed on in his Ascension, she too could not rest content with passing by but had to pass on in faith and devotion and follow him even to heaven. To believe in the Resurrection, then, is to pass by, but to believe in the Ascension is to pass on. Perhaps, as I remember saying one day, she knew the one, but not the other. Therefore their instruction had supplied the knowledge she lacked, that after the Resurrection he also ascended, and she likewise ascended. In fact, she passed on and she found him. How could she fail to find him, when she came in faith to where he is in the body? 'When I had left them behind a little while.'* And she is right to say 'them', for our head

Sg 3:4

has surpassed them as he has all his other
members* on earth, in two respects: in his
Resurrection, as we have seen, and in his
Ascension. Indeed 'Christ is the firstfruits'*—
he has gone before, and our faith has gone
with him. Where would it not follow him? If
he goes up to heaven, our faith is there; if he
goes down to hell, it is there. If he takes the
wings of the morning and dwells in the uttermost parts of the sea, even there your hand
will lead me and your right hand will hold
me.* Is it not then through our faith that
the omnipotent and good God has raised us
us and made us sit down at his right hand?*
This is to explain what the Church said, 'I left
them behind', for she has left herself behind,
abiding in faith* where she had not yet come
in fact. It must now be clear why she said she
had left them behind and passed on, rather
than met them as she passed. Let us go on to
the next words.

4. 'I have hold of him and will not let him
go until I bring him to my mother's house,
into the bedchamber of her who bore me.'*
And so it is; from that time onward the
christian people has never failed; there has
been faith on earth and charity within the
Church. 'Floods came, winds blew and beat
upon that house, but it did not fall, for it was
founded on a rock.'*   And the rock is
Christ.* Therefore neither the wordy utterances of philosophers, nor the wranglings of
heretics, nor the swords of persecutors, can
ever separate it from the love of God which
is in Christ Jesus.* So, firmly does she hold to
him whom her soul loves, so good it is

Col 3:5

1 Cor 15:23

Ps 138:8-10

Eph 2:6

Rom 11:20

Sg 3:4

Mt 7:25

1 Cor 10:4

Rom 8:39

to cling to God.* 'It is ready for the solder-   *Ps 72:28.*
ing', said Isaiah.* What holds more strongly   *Is 41:7*
than this solder, which is not washed away by
water, or blown away by the wind, or cleft by
the sword? 'Many waters cannot quench
love.'* 'I have hold of him and will not let him   *Sg 8:7*
go.'* And the holy patriarch Jacob said, 'I   *Sg 3:4*
will not let you go unless you bless me.'* So   *Gen 32:26*
she does not want to let him go, and perhaps
she is more determined than the patriarch,
for she does not want to let him go even for a
blessing. Now when Jacob had received a
blessing he let him go, but she would not. 'It
is not your blessing I desire', she says, 'but
you. What have I in heaven, and what do I
desire on earth apart from you? I will not let
you go, even if you bless me.'*   *Ps 72:25*

5. 'I have hold of him, and will not let
him go.' But perhaps he wishes to be held, for
he says, 'My delight is to be with the sons of
men',* and he promises, 'Lo, I am with you   *Prov 8:31*
every day, even 'til the end of the world.'*   *Mt 28:20*
What bond can be stronger than this, which is
secured by the single strong will of the two
who make it? 'I held him', she says. Yet in
her turn she is held by the one whom she
holds, and she says to him, 'You have held
me by the right hand.'* Now she both holds   *Ps 72:24*
and is held. How can she fall? She holds him
by her strong faith and devoted affection.
Yet she could not hold for long unless she
herself was held. She is held by the power and
mercy of God. 'I have hold of him and will
not let him go until I bring him to my
mother's house, into the bedchamber of her
who bore me.'* Great is the charity of the   *Sg 3:4*

Church, who does not grudge her delights
even to her rival, the Synagogue. What could
be kinder than to be willing to share with her
enemy him whom her soul loves? But it is not
surprising, because 'salvation is from the
Jews'.* The Saviour returned to the place
from which he had come, so that the remnant
of Israel might be saved.* Let not the
branches be ungrateful to the root, nor sons
to their mother; let not the branches grudge
the roots the sap they took from it, nor the
sons grudge their mother the milk they sucked
from her breast. Let the Church hold fast the
salvation which the Jews lost; she holds it until
the fulness of the Gentiles comes,* and so all
Israel may be saved. Let her wish that the
universal salvation come to all, for it can be
possessed by everyone without anyone having
less. This she does, and more, for she desires
for the Jews the name and grace of a Bride.
This is more than salvation.

6. This charity would be unbelievable,
but that the words of the Bride herself com-
pel belief. For you will observe that she said
she wished to bring him whom she held not
only to her mother's house but into her bedchamber, which is a mark of singular privilege.
For him to enter the house would be enough
for salvation; but the privacy of her bedchamber betokens grace, 'This day has salvation come to this house', said our Lord.
Salvation must necessarily come to a house
once the Saviour has entered it. But she who
is found worthy to receive him in the
bedchamber has a secret for herself alone.*

Jn 4:22

Rom 9:27

Rom 11:25-6

Qo 10:20

Salvation is for the house;* the bridal cham-   *Lk 19:9*
ber has its own secret delights.* 'I will bring   *Is 24:16*
him to my mother's house',* she says. What   *Sg 3:4*
house is this, unless it is the one fore-
shadowed to the Jews. 'Behold, your house
shall be left for you desolate.'* He has done   *Lk 13:35*
what he said, and you have his words in the
writings of the prophet: 'I have left my house
and my inheritance,'* and now she promises   *Jer 12:7*
to bring him back and restore its lost salvation to her mother's house. And if this is not
enough, hear the promise of good things which
she adds: 'and into the bedchamber of her
who bore me.'* He who enters the bridal   *Sg 3:4*
chamber is the bridegroom. How great is the
power of love! The Saviour had left his house
and his inheritance in anger; now he has
relented and inclined towards her in love, and
thus returns not only as Saviour but as Bridegroom. You are blessed by the Lord, O
daughter,* for you have softened his anger   *Jdth 13:23*
and restored the inheritance! You are blessed
by your mother, for it is through your blessing that his anger is turned away and salvation restored with him who says 'I am your
salvation'.* Nor is this enough. He goes on to   *Ps 34:3*
say, 'I will betrothe you to myself in justice
and righteousness; I will betrothe you to myself in mercy and pity.'* But remember that it   *Hos 2:20*
is the Bride who has brought about this recon-
ciliation. How can she give up her Bridegroom
to another, and choose to do it willingly? But
it is not so. She is a good daughter, and desires
to share him with her mother, not to give him
up. The one is enough for both, for they   *Mt 19:56*
are one in him.* He is our peace,† he who   *Eph 2:14*

Rom 9:5

made both one, that there might be one Bride and one Bridegroom, Jesus Christ our Lord, who is God above all, blessed for ever. Amen.*

SERMON EIGHTY

I. A RETURN TO THE MORAL LEVEL;
THE RELATIONSHIP BETWEEN THE SOUL
AND THE WORD. II. OF THE IMMEASUR-
ABLE SUPERIORITY OF THE WORD TO
THE SOUL, AND HOW GREATNESS AND
UPRIGHTNESS ARE NOT ONE WITH THE
SOUL AS THEY ARE WITH THE WORD.
III. THE REASONING BY WHICH THE
SOUL IS SHOWN TO BE DISTINCT FROM
ITS GREATNESS. IV. AGAINST THE PER-
VERSE DOCTRINE OF THOSE WHO SAY
THAT DIVINITY IS NOT GOD, AND OF
THE UNSOUNDNESS OF THE TREATISE
OF GILBERT OF POITIERS ON BOETHIUS'
ON THE TRINITY.

I. 1. **S**OME OF YOU, I hear, are resentful because for some days I have been regaling you by talking of the amazing and wonderful mysteries of God, yet the sermon I was giving savored too little if at all of moral considerations.* This is most unusual. But allow me to repair the omission. I cannot continue without completely cover- ing the subject. Tell me then, if you remem- ber, at what point I began this misuse of the Scriptures, so that I can go back to it. For it is for me to make good these losses, or rather it is for the Lord on whom we all

Col 4:6

145

depend. From what point then shall I begin?
Perhaps from this: 'In my little bed by night
I sought him whom my soul loves.'* I think
that must be the place, for from that point
on I had only one thought, to penetrate the
obscurity of these allegories and reveal the
secrets of Christ and his Church. Let us return
then to the search for the moral meaning, for
I cannot be indifferent to what is to your
advantage. And this task will be fitly undertaken if we consider the Word and the soul in
the same way in which we considered Christ
and the Church.*

2. But someone says to me, 'Why do you
take these two together? What have the Word
and the soul in common?' Much, on all
counts.* In the first place, there is a natural
kinship, in that the one is the Image of God,*
and the other is made in that image. Next,
their resemblance argues some affinity. For
the soul is made not only in the image*of
God* but in his likeness. In what does this
likeness consist? you ask. Take first the
Image. The word is truth, it is wisdom and
righteousness. These constitute the Image.
The image of what? Of righteousness, wisdom, and truth. For the image, the Word, is
righteousness from righteousness, wisdom
from wisdom, truth from truth, as he is light
and God from God.* The soul is none of these
things, since it is not the image. Yet it is
capable of them and yearns for them; that
perhaps is why it is said to be made in the
image. It is a lofty creature, in its capacity
for greatness, and in its longing we see a token
of its uprightness. We read that God made

Sg 3:1

Eph 5:32

Rom 3:2
Col 1:15

Gen 1:27
Gen 5:2

Cf. Nicaean Creed

man upright* and great; his capacity proves   *Qo 7:30*
that, as we have said. For what is made in the
image should conform to the image, and not
merely share the empty name of image—as
the image [of God] himself is not merely
called by the empty name of image. You
know that it is said of him who is the image
of God that although he was in the form of
God, he did not think it robbery to be equal
with God.* You see that his uprightness is   *Phil 2:6*
indicated because he is in the form of God,
and his greatness in his equality with God, so
that in the comparison of uprightness with
uprightness and greatness with greatness, it
appears on two accounts that what is made
in the image agrees with the image, just as the
image also corresponds in both respects to that
of which it is the image. For he is the one of
whom you have heard holy David sing in his
Psalm 'Great is the Lord, and great is his
power';* and again 'The Lord our God is   *Ps 146:5*
upright, and in him there is no unrighteousness.'* He is the image of this upright and   *Ps 91:16*
great God; therefore the soul which is in his
image is like him.

II. 3. But I ask: Is there no difference
between the image of God and the soul
which is made in its image, since we attribute
greatness and uprightness to it, too? Indeed
there is. For the soul receives according to its
capacity, but the image receives in equal
measure with God. Is there no more to say?
You must mark this as well: the soul is
endowed with both by God who created him
and made him great, but the image of God

receives them by God's begetting. And who can deny that this is a much greater dignity.' Although man received his gifts from God's hands,* the image received them from God's being,* that is from his very substance. For the image of God is of the same substance as God, and everything which he seems to share with his image is part of the substance of both, and not accident. There is yet one more thing to be considered, in which the image is no less superior. Everyone knows that greatness and righteousness are distinct in their nature, but in the image they are one. Furthermore they are one with him who is the image. For the image, greatness is not merely the same as uprighteousness, but existence itself is greatness and uprightness. It is not so with the soul; its greatness and uprightness are distinct from it and distinct from each other. But if, as I argued before, the soul is great in proportion to its capacity for the eternal, and upright in proportion to its desire for heavenly things, then the soul which does not desire or have a taste for heavenly things, but clings to earthly things,* is clearly not upright but bent, but it does not for all this cease to be great, and it always retains its capacity for eternity. For even if it never attains to it it never ceases to be capable of doing so, and so the Scripture is fulfilled. Truly man 'passes as an image',* yet only in part, so that the superiority of the Word may be seen in its completeness. For how can the Word fail to be great and upright, since it possesses these qualities as part of its nature? Man possesses these gifts in part also because if he were

a Deo

de Deo

Col 3:2

Ps 38:7

completely deprived of them there would be
no hope of salvation,* for if he ceased to be
great he would lose his capacity, and, as I have
said, the soul's greatness is measured by its
capacity. What hope of salvation could there
be for one who had no capacity for receiving it?

4. And so by the greatness which it
retains even when it has lost its uprightness,
'man passes as an image', but he limps, as it
were, on one foot, and has become an
estranged son. Of someone like this, it can,
I think, be said: 'the estranged sons have lied
to me, they have become weak, and have
limped away from the path.'* They are well
called 'estranged sons', for they are sons
inasmuch as they keep their greatness, and
estranged because they have lost their uprightness. If they had completely lost the
image, the psalmist would not have said 'they
have fallen away' or some such thing. But
now 'man passes as an image' because of his
greatness; but as far as his uprightness is concerned, he limps, he is troubled, and he is
torn away from the image. As Scripture says:
'Truly man passes as an image; he is troubled
in vain.'* Utterly in vain; for he goes on to
say, 'He piles up riches and does not know for
whom he gathers it.'* Why does he not
know, unless because he is bending down to
the ground,* the earth which he heaps up for
himself? Also, he does not know for whom he
is piling up the riches he is committing to the
earth. It may be devoured by the moth, dug
up by a thief,* stolen by an enemy,† or
destroyed by fire.* So it is to the unhappy

Acts 27:30

Ps 17:46

Jn 8:6

Ps 38:7

Jn 8:6

*Mt 6:19
†Deut 9:3

*Is 30:27

man who is bending and brooding over earthly things that the melancholy voice from Psalms refers: 'I am troubled. I am bowed down to the earth. I go in sadness all the day long.'* He has experienced the truth of the saying of the Preacher: 'God made man upright, but he is bowed down by many troubles.'* Then immediately afterwards he is told mockingly, 'Bow down, so that we may walk over you.'*

Ps 37:7

Qo 7:30

Is 51:23

III. 5. But how have we arrived here? Was it not that we wished to show that uprightness and greatness, the two virtues we had descried in the image, were not one in the soul or with the soul, as we showed in our declaration of faith that they are one in the Word and with the Word. It is clear from what we have said that uprightness is distinct from the soul and from the greatness of the soul, since even when it does not exist the soul remains, and is still great. But how can it be proved that the greatness of the soul is distinct from the soul? It cannot be proved as the diversity of the soul and its uprightness was proved, since the soul cannot be deprived of its greatness as it can be of its uprightness. Yet its greatness is not the soul; for even if the soul is never found apart from its greatness, yet that greatness is found outside the soul. You ask where? In the angels, for the greatness of the angels derives from the same source as the greatness of the soul, from its capacity for the things of eternity. For if we agree that the soul is distinct from its righteousness, in that it can exist without it, can it not be assumed that it is also distinct from its greatness, which it cannot claim as its own property? And since the one is not found in every soul, and the other is found otherwise than in the soul, it is obvious that each without distinction is distinct from the soul. Likewise that of which the soul is the form has no form, whereas its greatness is the form of the soul. It must be its form when it is inseparable from it. All differences between substances are of this kind, both those which are proper to one thing exclusively and those which have many different forms. The soul itself does not consist of its greatness, any more than a crow consists of its blackness or snow of its whiteness, or a man of his ability to laugh or his ability to reason, but you never find a crow without blackness, or a man devoid of the ability to laugh and to reason. So the soul and the greatness of the soul are inseparable, yet they are distinct from each other. How can they be other than inseparable, since the one is the subject and the other the substance? Only that supreme and un-created nature, which is God the Holy Trinity, reserves for itself this pure and unique simplicity of essence, that there is not found in it one thing and another thing, in one place and another place, at one time and another time. It dwells in itself; it is what possesses and what it is, always & unchangingly. In the Trinity many diverse qualities are united, so that it does not suffer plurality as a result of multiplicity of elements, nor change as a result of variety. It contains all places, and not being contained in anything, sets all things in

order. All time is subject to it, not it to time.
it does not await the future, or look back at
the past, or experience the present.

IV. 6. Beloved, beware of those who teach
new doctrines, who are not logicians but
heretics, who blasphemously argue that the
greatness by which God is great,* the goodness by which he is good, the righteousness by
which he is righteous, and finally the divinity
by which he is God, are not God. 'God', they
say, 'is God by reason of his divinity, but the
divinity is not God.'[1] Perhaps it does not
condescend to be God, because it is what
makes God what he is? But if it is not God,
what is it? Either it is God, or it is something
which is not God, or it is nothing. Now you
do not admit that it is God, nor, I think, will
you argue that it is nothing; but you make
out that it is so necessary to God that not
only can God not be God without it, but by
it he is God. But if it is something which is
not God, either it will be less than God, or
greater, or equal to him. How can it be less, if
by it God is God? You must then postulate
that it is greater, or equal. If it is greater, it is
itself the highest good, but it is not God. If it
is equal to God, there are two beings which
are the highest good, not one; but the
Catholic faith rejects both these conclusions.
Now we hold the same beliefs about his greatness, his goodness, his righteousness and his

---

1. *Divinitate Deus est; sed divinitas non est Deus.* See N. M. Häring,
'The Case of Gilbert de la Porrée, Bishop of Poitiers (1142-1154),
Mediaeval Studies 13 (1951) 1-40, esp. 12-13.

wisdom as we do about his divinity, that they
are all one in God and with God. Nor does his
goodness come from any other source than
his greatness, nor his righteousness nor his
wisdom from any other source than his greatness and goodness; nor do all these attributes
together have any other origin than his
divinity, nor do they exist apart from him.

7. But the heretic says 'What? Do you
deny that God is so by his divinity?' No; but I
allege that the divinity by which God is God
is itself God, lest I make out that anything is
more excellent than God. For I maintain that
God is great by reason of his greatness, but is
himself that greatness. Otherwise I might be
setting something else above God; and I con-
fess that he is good by his goodness, but it
does not exist apart from him. Otherwise I
might seem to have found something better
than he; and so on with regard to other
attributes. I go on my way in freedom and
safety, without stumbling, as they say, hold-
ing the view of him who said, 'God is great
with the greatness which is himself, otherwise
the greatness would be greater than God'.
Augustine that was, that mighty hammer of
heretics. If this can be properly predicted of
God, it can also be said, 'God is greatness,
goodness, righteousness, and wisdom' even
more correctly and with greater reason than
saying, 'God is great, good, righteous, and
wise'.

8. It is not without cause, therefore, that
Pope Eugenius himself and the other bishops
at the recent Council at Reims condemned
the exposition made by Gilbert, Bishop of

Poitiers, in his commentary on Boethius' treatise *On the Trinity,* a very sound and orthodox
work.[2] This is what Gilbert said: 'The Father
is truth, that is, he is true; the Son is truth,
that is, he is true; the Holy Spirit is truth,
that is, he is true. And these three are not
three truths but one truth, that is, one being
who is true.'[3] What an obscure and confused
explanation! How much nearer the truth, and
how much more reasonable, to have said, on
the other hand: 'The Father is true, that is, he
is truth; the Son is true, that is, he is truth;
the Holy Spirit is true, that is, he is truth. And
these three are one being who is true, that is,
they are one truth.' This is what he would
have said if he had been content to echo the
teaching of Fulgentius; 'There is one truth, of
one God, or rather there is one truth which is
one God, who does not allow the service and
worship due to the Creator to be confused

Fulgentius of with what can be given to the creature.'*
Ruspe, Letter 8.12; He was a good teacher, and spoke truly of the
PL 65:65D-66A.
truth; he had reverent and orthodox opinions
about the true and pure simplicity of the
divine substance, in which there can be
nothing but itself, and itself is God. There
are sundry other passages in this book in
which the aforesaid bishop is clearly at
variance with the true teaching of the Faith,

2. *De Trinitate,* edited and translated by H. F. Stewart and E. K.
Rand, *Boethius: The Theological Tractates* (London–Cambridge, MA:
The Loeb Classical Library, 1918).
3. *In Boethium de Trinitate* 2.1.27; ed. by N. M. Häring, *Studies
and Texts, 1* (Toronto: The Pontifical Institute of Mediaeval Studies,
1955), p. 94.

and I will adduce one of these. When Boethius said, 'God, God, God—refers to the substance',[4] this commentator of ours adds: 'Not what [the substance] is but by which it is what it is.'[5] God forbid that the Church should give assent to the proposition that there is any substance, or any other thing, by which God is what he is, but which is not God.

9. I am not speaking against him personally, for in the same council he gave humble assent to the Bishops' pronouncements when they found this and other passages deserving of censure, and he retracted them with his own mouth. I am speaking against those who are apparently still copying out and poring over this book, contrary to the apostolic prohibition promulgated in that same Council, following the Bishop with obstinate insistence in opinions he has disclaimed, and preferring to have him as their instructor in error rather than in its correction. As we are considering the difference between the image and the soul, I thought it worth taking the opportunity to make this digression, not only for its own sake but for yours, so that if any of you had at any time drunk forbidden waters, which seem to taste sweeter,* they *Prov 9:17* might take the antidote and disgorge them, and come with cleansed minds to that which remains to be said, according to the promise I made, about the likeness of the soul to the

4. Cf. Boethius, *De Trin.* (Loeb, 22), Gilbert, *In Boet.* 1.9.4, and 1.4.1 (Häring, 76,62).

5. Gilbert, *In Boet.* 1.9.4 (76). Cf. Boethius, *De Trin.* IV (22).

Is 12:3

Word, and may drink joyfully,* not of my fountain, but of that of the Saviour, the Bridegroom of the Church, Jesus Christ our Lord, who is God above all, blessed for ever.

Rom 9:5

Amen.*

SERMON EIGHTY-ONE

I. THE LIKENESS OF THE SOUL TO THE
WORD IS MOST PARTICULARLY SHOWN
IN THAT FOR THE SOUL BEING IS LIVING,
AS FOR THE WORD BEING IS LIVING IN
BLESSEDNESS. II. OF THE DIFFERENT
KINDS OF LIVING CREATURES; HOW
ONLY FOR THE SOUL IS TO BE TO LIVE,
AND WHAT THE SOUL RECEIVES IN THIS
CONDITION. III. OF THE IMMORTALITY
OF THE SOUL, WHICH IS NOT LIKE THAT
OF THE WORD; ITS THREEFOLD AFFIN-
ITY TO THE WORD, IN SIMPLICITY, PER-
PETUITY, AND LIBERTY, AND IN WHAT
ITS LIBERTY CONSISTS. IV. HOW THE
SOUL'S LIBERTY IS CURTAILED BY SIN.
V. OF THE LAW OF GOD AND THE LAW
OF SIN, WHICH IN THE SOUL ARE ALSO
IDENTICAL IN WILL.

I. 1. IT WAS NOT WITHOUT REASON
that we investigated the affinity of
the soul to the Word. What can there
be in common between majesty so great and
poverty so extreme* that such sublimity and
such lowliness should be considered as though
they were associated on equal terms? If we
say that truly, we can indeed be confident
and joyful; but if falsely, then such insolence
deserves severe punishment. Therefore we had

Cf. 2 Cor 6:15

to investigate the affinity between them; and
we have examined many aspects of this, but
not all. No one can be so blind that he does

Col 1:15 not see the resemblance between the image*

Gen 1:27 and what is made in the image.* Yesterday's
sermon, if you remember, made a clear distinction between the two, and we not only
dealt with that but also mentioned their great

Gen 5:3 similarity.* But we have not yet considered
the nature of that similarity, or its more
important aspects. Let us now proceed to
consider this point, that the more fully the
soul recognizes its origin, the more it will
blush for the unworthiness of its life—more
than this, it will be anxious to make every
effort to reform what it sees in its nature to be
deformed by sin, so that by God's help it may
rule itself in a way worthy of its origin, and
faithfully approach the Word's enfolding.

2. Let it be aware, then, that because of
its origin in the divine likeness it has in itself a
natural simplicity of substance by which for
it to exist is to live, even if it does not imply

beate vivere living in a state of blessedness;* its likeness does
not imply equality. This is a degree, of like-
ness, but only a degree; it is not synonymous
with living in a state of blessedness, which is
the prerogative of the highest virtue. If therefore this quality of life is the prerogative of
the Word, by reason of the perfection of its
nature, life is the prerogative of the soul
because of its natural affinity to the Word. To
make this clearer: it is for God alone that to
be is synonymous with being in a state of
blessedness, and this is the first and purest

Mt 22:39 simplicity. The second is similar to it,*

namely, that existence is living, and this is the prerogative of the soul; and even if it is a lower degree, it can be raised not only to living well, but even to living blessedly. But even for the soul which attains to this to be is not the same thing as to be blessed, since it is glorified by its likeness to the Word, yet because of its distinction between them it will always have to say 'Lord, who is like you?' It is a degree of advancement for the soul, from which alone it may rise to the blessed life.*

Ps 34:10

II. 3. There are two kinds of living beings, those which have consciousness and those which do not.* The sensate rank above the insensate, and above them both is life, by which one lives and is conscious. Life and living beings do not rank equally; much less life and lifeless things. Life is the living soul, but it does not derive its life from any other source than itself; strictly speaking, we describe this as life rather than living. Thus it follows that when this is infused into the soul it gives it life, so that the body, through the presence of life, becomes not life itself but a living thing. From this it is clear that, even for a living body, to be is not the same as to live. Much less do those things which are without life attain to this degree. Not even will everything which is described as life, or which is indeed so, be able to reach that point. There is a life of cattle and of trees, the first conscious, the second lacking consciousness. For neither of these does being involve living, since, according to many people, their existence has been in the elements before it was

sentiunt ... non sentiunt

in their limbs. But according to this view, when they cease to quicken they cease to live, but not to be. They are dissolved and separated, as though they had been not only bound together but mingled. For they are not one simple organism but are compounded of several. Therefore it is not reduced to nothing* but dissolved into its component parts, and each returns to its first principle; for example, air returns to air, fire to fire, and so forth. For such a quality of life to be is by no means the same as to live; it is even when it does not live.

Job 16:8, 17:7, 30:15

4. Now none of such things, to which being is not the same thing as living, will ever make progress or rise, since it could not reach even the lower degree. The soul of man alone, which is recognized as being established in it, was created with this dignity, life from life, simple from the simple, immortal from the immortal, so that he is not far from the highest degree, where to be is synonymous with living in blessedness, in which abides the blessed and only powerful King of kings and Lord of lords.* The soul by its condition has received the capability of being blessed, even if it is not yet blessed, and it is approaching that highest degree as far as it can, yet without reaching it. For as we said above, even when it attains blessedness, this will not be the same for it as being blesséd. There is a similarity, I admit, but I reject any idea of equality. For example, God is life and the soul is life; it is like him, then, but it is not equal. Moreover, it is like him because it is life, because its life is within itself, because it

1 Tim 6:15

is not only a living thing but a lifegiving thing,
just as God himself is all these things; but it is
unlike him as a creature is unlike its creator,
and unlike because if it had not been
quickened by God it would not live. I say it
would not live, but I refer to its spiritual life,
not its natural one. It must live immortally on
the natural, even if it does not on the
spiritual plane. But what kind of life would it
be in which it would be better not to be born
than not to die? It is death rather than life,
and the more grievous in that it is the death
of sin, not of nature. For the death of sinners
is very evil.* Thus the soul which lives [Ps 33:22]
according to the flesh* is dead though it lives, [Rom 8:13]
for it would have been better for it never to
have lived than to live in such a way.* And it [1 Tim 5:6]
will never rise from that living death except
through the Word of life, or rather through
the Word which is life, both living and
life-giving.* [Eph 5:26]

III. 5. Now the soul is immortal, and in this
it is also similar, but not equal to, the Word.
For the immortality of the Godhead is so far
above it that the Apostle says of God, 'He
who alone possesses immortality'.* This was [1 Tim 6:16]
said of him, I think, because only God is by
nature unchangeable—he said 'I am God, and
I do not change'.* For true and integral [Mal 3:6]
immortality does not admit change any more
than it does ending, because all change is in
some way an imitation of death. Everything
which changed, in passing from one state to
another, necessarily dies to what it is, so that
it may begin to be what it is not. But if

every change necessarily involves death, where is immortality? 'For the creature was made subject to vanity, not of its own will, but of that of him whom made it; yet it has hope.'* But the soul is immortal, and since it has life in itself, and there is no way in which it can fall away from itself, so there is no way in which it can fall away from life. But it is plain that it changes in its affections and it so recognizes that its likeness to God in its immortality is incomplete that it realizes it lacks no small part of immortality. It acknowledges that absolute and complete immortality is seen in God alone, in whom is no change nor shadow of alteration.* But it has been established in the present discussion that the soul has no little dignity, since it seems to resemble the Word in two respects: simplicity of essence and perpetuity of life.

6. But one point has occurred to me which I cannot neglect, and which in no way detracts from the soul's greatness and its similarity to the Word, but enhances them. This is free choice, something clearly divine which shines forth in the soul like a jewel set in gold. From it the soul derives its power of judgment, and its option of choosing between good and evil, between life and death, in fact between light and darkness, and any other concepts which are perceived by the soul as opposites. It is the eye of the soul which as censor and arbiter exercises discrimination and discernment between these things, and arbiter in discerning and free in choosing. It is called free choice because it is exercised in these matters in accordance with the freedom of the will.

Rom 8:20

Jm 1:17

By it a man can acquire merit; everything you do, whether good or ill, which you had the choice of doing or not doing, is duly imputed to you for merit or censure. And as a man is rightly praised for refraining from doing wrong when he might have done wrong,* so also someone who could have *Si 31:10* refrained from doing wrong but did wrong, like someone who could have done right but did not do so, is not free from censure. But when there is no freedom, there is no merit or blame. Therefore animals devoid of reason gain no merit, for they lack deliberation just as they lack freedom. They are prompted by the senses, led by impulse, dominated by appetite. They have no judgment to rule their actions, nor any faculty for exercising judgment, which is reason. It follows that they can incur no judgment since they exercise none. How can they reasonably be expected to exercise a faculty of reason which they have not received?

IV. 7. It is only man who has not thus been dominated by nature, therefore he alone among living creatures is free. Yet when sin intervenes, even man is dominated, but by his will, not by nature, and he is not thereby deprived of the liberty which is his birthright. What is done willingly is done freely. It is by sin that the corruptible body oppresses the soul,* but it is the result of love, not of force. *Wis 9:15* For although the soul fell of itself, it cannot rise of itself, because the will lies weak and powerless through the vitiated and depraved love of a corrupt body, yet is at the same

time capable of a love of justice. So, in some
strange and twisted way the will deteriorates
and brings about a state of compulsion where
bondage cannot excuse the will, because the
action was voluntary, nor can the will, being
fettered, free itself from bondage. For this
bondage is in some sense voluntary. It is an
agreeable bondage which flatters while it
overcomes, and overcomes by flattery, so that
when the will has betrayed itself by consenting
to sin, it cannot of itself throw off the yoke,
nor reasonably excuse itself. Then, like the
voice of one groaning under the yoke of bondage, 'comes this cry, "Lord, I am oppressed;
answer for me'.* But now listen to what
he says next, knowing that he has no just
complaint against the Lord, since it was his
own will which was to blame: 'What am I to
say? Who will speak for me? For I myself have
done this evil.'* He was oppressed by the
yoke, but the yoke of a voluntary servitude;
because it was servitude, he is miserable, yet
because it was voluntary, inexcusable. For it
is the will which, although free, by consenting
to sin became slave to sin; and it is the will
which puts itself in subjection to sin by its
willing servitude.

8. 'Take care what you say,' someone will
reply, 'You say it is willing, but it is obviously
in bondage.' It is true that the will gave its
consent, but it does not keep itself there; it is
kept there against its will. You must agree
that it is being held. But remember that it is
the will which you state is held. Do you say
that the will is unwilling? The will is not kept
against its will. The will is that of a willing

Is 38:14

Is 38:15

man, not an unwilling one. But if it is kept willingly, it is keeping itself back. What will it say, or who will answer for it, since it has itself done this thing?* What has it done? It has enslaved itself. Therefore it is said: 'He who comments sin is a slave to sin.'* So when it sins—and when it sins it has determined to obey sin—it enslaves itself. It would be free if it no longer committed sin; but it does so, thus keeping itself in that same servitude. The will is not held against its will, for it is the will, therefore because it is willing, it has not only enslaved itself, but continues to do so. It deserves, then, and this must be borne in mind—to ask who will be its surety, since it has itself sinned and continues to do so.*

9. 'But', you say, 'you will not make me deny the bondage which I suffer, which I experience in myself and against which I struggle continually.' 'Where do you experience this bondage?' I ask. 'Is it not in the will? Your will is not diminished because it is in bondage. Your will is strong to do what you cannot refuse to do, even if you struggle. Now where there is will there is freedom.' But I speak of natural freedom, not spiritual, by which, as the Apostle says, Christ has set us free.* He also it was who said, 'Where the spirit is, there is freedom.'* So the soul, in a strange and evil way, is both held as a slave in this voluntary and yet irresistible bondage, and it is free. It is enslaved and free at the same time; enslaved through bondage, free because of its will,* and, which is even stranger and more unfortunate, guilty in proportion to its freedom, and enslaved in

Ibid.

Jn 8:34

Is 38:15

Gal 4:31
2 Cor 3:17

Gal 4:22

Rom 7:24

Job 7:20

Ibid.

Rom 7:23

Cf. Rom 7:24,
15-16

Ps 70:4

proportion to its guilt, and therefore enslaved in proportion to its freedom. Unhappy man that I am, who will deliver me from the shame of this bondage?* Unhappy I may be, but I am free. I am free because I am a man, unhappy because I am a slave. I am free because I am like God, unhappy because I am in opposition to God. 'O watcher of men, why have you set me against you?'* For this is what you did, when you did not stop me. But at the same time it was I who set myself against you, and 'I have become a burden to myself'.* It is indeed just that your enemy should be my enemy, and that someone who opposes you opposes me. But it is I who am against you, I who have become my own enemy, and I find in myself that which is in opposition both to my mind and to your law.*

V. Who will set me free from my own hands? 'What I wish to do, that I do not' and it is I myself, not another, who frustrates me—'and that which I hate, that I do'.* But it is I myself, not someone else, who compels me to do it. Would that this frustration, this compulsion, were so strong that it was not voluntary, then perhaps I might be excused; if it were to be voluntary to the extent that it was less powerful, then I might be corrected. But now, alas, there is no way of escape open to me, for, as I have said, my possession of a will robs me of excuse, & the bondage I endure robs me of the possibility of correction. Who will snatch me from the hand of the sinner,* from the hand of the evil-doer and the wicked man?

10. 'Who are you complaining about?'
someone asks. About myself. It is I who am
that sinner, that outlaw, that wicked man.
I am the sinner, for it is I who have sinned.
I am the outlaw, because of my own will I
persist in breaking the law. For my will itself
is a law in my members* which rebels against   *Rom 7:23*
the divine law. And since the law of the
Lord is the law of my mind it is written, 'the
law of God is in his heart'*—my very will is   *Ps 36:31*
seen to be against me; and this is complete loss
of integrity. For if I am untrue to myself, I
am untrue to everyone. If a man injures himself, how can he benefit anyone?* I admit I   *Si 14:5*
am not good, because there is no good in me.
But I shall find comfort in the word of the
saint: 'I know that in me there is no good,'
he said.* But he makes a distinction when he   *Rom 7:18*
says 'in him', explaining that he refers to the
flesh, because of the perversity of the law
within it. For there is a law in the mind as
well, and a better one. Is the law of God not
good? If wickedness is due to the law of
wickedness, goodness must be due to the law
of goodness. Is the law in a man's flesh evil,
and does its evil spring from the evil law
within it, and yet a man is not good because
the law of goodness? It is not so: the law of
God is in his mind,* and in his mind in such a   *Cf. Ps 36:31*
way as to be the law of his mind. Witness
[Saint Paul,] who says, 'I find one law in my
body, warring against the law of my mind.*   *Rom 7:23*
Can what is in his flesh be his own, and what
is in his mind not be his own? It is indeed his
own, even more. Why should I not echo the
words of this same teacher? 'With my mind I

Rom 7:25

Rom 7:20

Rom 7:25

Rom 7:20

Gra IX.28-35
(CF 19:84-92)

obey the law of God, but in my flesh I obey the law of sin.'* He shows clearly what he admits to be his own when he dismisses the evil in his flesh as foreign to him. He says, 'Now it is not I who act, but the sin dwelling within me'.* Perhaps he said that he found another law in his members precisely because he thought this was foreign to him, coming as it were from outside him. Therefore I venture to go further, but not imprudently, and say that Paul was not evil because of the evil in his flesh so much as he was good because of the good within his mind. Is a man not good when he consents to the law of God, since that is good? Even if he acknowledges that he is enslaved to the law of sin, it is in the flesh that he is so, not in the mind. Since, however, he serves the law of God in his mind* but the law of sin in his flesh, you can see for yourselves which of these should be considered more characteristic of Paul. I admit that what is of the mind is greater than what is of the flesh, and this is not only my view but that of Paul, too, as he expressed it in the words I have already quoted: 'What I wish to do, that I do not; yet it is not I who act thus, but the sin which dwells within me.'*

11. Let that be enough about freedom. In the book I have written on grace and free choice you may find other observations about the image and the likeness,* but I do not think they contradict the things I have been saying. You have read them, and you have heard what I have just said; I leave it to your judgement which is preferable. If you find

anything worth remembering in either, I am pleased, and shall always be so.* However that may be, remember that I have particularly mentioned three qualities: simplicity, immortality, and freedom. And I think it must be clear to you that through its inborn likeness, which illuminates these qualities, the soul has a great affinity with the Word, the Bridegroom of the Church, Jesus Christ our Lord, who is God above all, blessed for ever. Amen.*

Phil 1:18

Rom 9:5

SERMON EIGHTY-TWO

I. WHAT IS STILL OBSCURE IN WHAT HAS
BEEN SAID, AND MUST BE ELUCIDATED,
AND HOW A CERTAIN MAN HEARD A
VOICE SAYING, 'AS LONG AS YOU HOLD
THAT BACK' ETC. II. OF GOD'S LIKE-
NESS IN MAN, WHICH APPEARS, ACCORD-
ING TO CERTAIN PASSAGES OF SCRIP-
TURE, TO BE DESTROYED BY SIN; THAT
IT MUST BE REGARDED AS DARKENED
AND CONFUSED, IN REGARD TO SIMPLI-
CITY AS WELL AS TO IMMORTALITY AND
FREEDOM, AND HOW THIS CAME ABOUT.
III. OF THE ACCIDENTAL EVILS WHICH
DEFILE THE NATURAL GIFTS OF THE
SOUL, AS A RESULT OF WHICH THE SAME
FATE COMES TO MEN AND BEASTS; BUT
BECAUSE OF ITS ENDURING LIKENESS IT
CAN HAVE RECOURSE TO THE WORD.

Mt 18:12

I. 1. **W**HAT DO YOU THINK?* Shall we return to our exposition at the point where we digressed, that is, the affinity between the Word and the soul? We might do that, I think, were it not that I have the impression that you have still some little uncertainty about what has *Ps 121:1* been said.* I do not wish to deprive you of anything, so I would not willingly pass over anything I thought might be of value to you.

170

Indeed, I would not dare to do that, especially in matters which I hold in trust for you. I know a man* who, in the course of a sermon, kept something back which the Spirit was putting into his mind, not because he distrusted the Spirit so much as because he lacked complete confidence, and wanted to save something to be sure to have something to say later. He seemed to hear a voice saying to him, 'As long as you hold that back you will receive no more'. Supposing he had kept it back, not as an insurance against his own inadequacy, but because he grudged advancement to his brethren, would he not deserve to have taken from him even what he seemed to have*? May God keep your servant from such a thing, as he always has done. So the unfailing fountain of saving wisdom* will deign to spring forth for me, since I have always shared everything with you ungrudgingly,* and whatever he has condescended to pour out for me I have poured out again for you. If I defrauded you, how could I expect not to be defrauded by others, even by God?

2. Now there is one point made which I fear may cause offence unless it is explained. If I am not mistaken, there are some standing here* who will be somewhat irritated by what I have to say. Do you remember that when I attributed to the soul a threefold likeness to the Word, I said it would be more accurate to say it was impressed into the soul? Now this may seem to conflict with some passages in the Scriptures, as, for example, that one in the Psalms: 'Although a man is held in honor,

2 Cor 12:2-3

Mt 25:29

Prov 18:4

Wis 7:13

Mt 16:27

Ps 48:21

Ps 105:20

Ps 49:21

Rom 8:31

he has no understanding; he is compared to foolish beasts and has become like them;'* and again: 'They changed their glory into the likeness of a calf who eats hay'*, and what has been said plainly by the Person of God: 'You thought, wicked man, that I was like you.'* There are many other passages which seem to state that God's likeness in man was utterly destroyed by sin. What shall we say to that?* Are we to deny that these attributes exist in God at all, and say that we must look for others in which to find this likeness? Or can we say that they do exist in the soul, but not necessarily, and therefore they are not inseparable from it? Far from it. They do exist both in God and in the soul, and do so always. And we need have no regrets for anything we have said; it is all supported by unquestionable and absolute truth.

II. Now when Holy Scripture speaks of the unlikeness that has come about, it says not that the likeness has been destroyed, but concealed by something else which has been laid over it. The soul has not in fact put off its original form but has put on one foreign to it. The latter is an addition; the former has not been lost. This addition can hide the original form, but it cannot blot it out. The Apostle Paul said, 'Their foolish heart was darkened',* and the Prophet Jeremiah said, 'How has the gold grown dim, and its pure color faded?'* The gold laments that it has grown dim, but it is still gold; its pure color is faded, but the base of the color is not altered. The simplicity of the soul remains

Rom 1:21

Lam 4:1

unshaken in its fundamental being, but it is
not seen because it is covered by the disguise
of human deception, pretence, and hypocrisy.
3. How incongruous is the mixture of simplicity and duplicity! How unworthy is so base
an addition to so pure a foundation! This was
the kind of duplicity which the serpent used
when he offered himself as a counsellor,
making out that he was a friend.* And when
the inhabitants of paradise were seduced by
him, this was what they put on in their
attempt to cover their embarrassing naked-
ness with the shade of a leafy tree, an apron
of leaves, and words of excuse. How widely
has the poisonous infection of deceit spread
through all their posterity ever since that
time! Which of the sons of Adam can you
think of who can bear, much less wish, to be
seen for what he is? Yet the original simplicity persists in every soul along with the
duplicity, and the co-existence of these increases the confusion. Its immortality continues also, but in an obscure and debased
form, with the dark clouds of physical death
of the body overshadowing it.* For although
it is not deprived of life, yet the gift of life
cannot preserve it in the body. What shall
I say of anyone who does not even preserve
the life of his spirit? 'The soul that sins shall
die.'* Now when that two-fold death comes
upon it, whatever immortality it retains is
surely somewhat gloomy and unhappy. Its
attachment to earthly things—which all tend
to destruction—makes the darkness deeper,
until a soul which lives this way has only a
pallid appearance, the very image of death.

Gen 3:1-5

Job 10:21

Ez 18:4

Why does the soul, being immortal, not desire
things which, like itself, are immortal and
eternal, so that it may appear as what it
really is, and live the life for which it was
made? But it finds its pleasure in things which
are contrary to these, and desires them, giving
its allegiance to transitory things. Thus its life
is debased and the brightness of immortality is
darkened by the dingy defilement of its perni-
cious way of life. Why then do the passions
treat something which is immortal as though
it were mortal, and turn it into something
quite unlike its immortal self? 'The man who
touches pitch', says the Preacher, 'will be

Si 13:1

defiled by it.'* By its taste for things which
are mortal it clothes itself in mortality; but
its robe of immortality, though stained with
the likeness of death, has not been cast away.

4. Consider Eve, and how her immortal
soul of immortal glory was infected by the
stain of mortality through her desire for mortal things. Why did she not spurn mortal and
transitory things, when she was immortal, and
satisfy herself with the immortal and eternal
things which were proper to her? 'She saw
that the tree was pleasing to the eyes and
pleasant to look upon and its fruit sweet to

Gen 3:6

to the taste',* that is what the Scriptures say.
But that sweetness, pleasantness and beauty is
not yours, O woman. Even if it is yours in the
sense that you also are part of the earth, it is
not yours alone, but you have it in common

Gen 2:19

with all living creatures.* What is truly yours
is of a different kind, and comes from a different source, for it is eternal and comes from
eternity. Why do you imprint upon your soul

a different form—or rather deformity? For
what it delights to possess, it fears to lose,
and this fear is a stain which colors and
covers its freedom, and makes it like itself.
How much more worthy of its divine origin
if it were free from desire and fear, and thus
preserved the freedom which is its birthright, and kept its pristine strength and
beauty! Alas, it is not so. Its pure color is
faded.* You run away, you go into hiding, *Lam 4:1*
you hear the voice of the Lord God,* and *Gen 3:8*
you hide yourself. Why do you do this except
because you fear him whom you used to love,
and the splendor of your freedom has been
swept away & replaced by the form of a slave?
   5. Now this necessity, incurred volun-
tarily, and the rebellious law which has descended upon the members,* which I spoke *Rom 7:23*
of in the last sermon, weighs upon that freedom, and binds the creature which is free by
nature, subjecting it to slavery by its own
will. Then it covers it with ignominy,* so *Ps 82:17*
that it will serve the law of sin* in its flesh, *Rom 7:25*
though unwillingly. Thus it has neglected to
protect its natural purity by innocence of life.
It is not thereby stripped of its freedom, but,
by the righteous judgment of its creator, it is
covered with confusion as with a cloak.* It *Ps 108:29*
is well said 'as with a cloak', which is a garment which is folded, for as the soul retains
its freedom by virtue of the will, yet it con-
ducts itself as a slave; and this imposes compulsion on it. What is said of the immortality
of the soul may also be said of its simplicity
and, if you reflect, you will find nothing in
that which is not similarly covered with the

folds of likeness and unlikeness. Is deceit not like the folds of a cloak, being not inborn but put on and, so to speak, with the needle of sin stitched on to simplicity, as death is to immortality, and compulsion to freedom? Duplicity of heart does not wipe out essential simplicity; nor does death—whether the voluntary death due to sin or the necessary death of the body—destroy the immortality of nature; again, the compulsion of voluntary servitude does not extinguish free will.

III. So these evils are accidental, and do not result from the good gifts which are natural, but are superimposed on them; they defile but do not wipe them out; they bring confusion upon them, but not destruction. So it is that the soul is unlike God and consequently unlike itself as well. So it is that it is compared to foolish beasts, and indeed becomes like them.* So it is that we read that its glory is changed into the likeness of a calf that eats hay.* So it is that men, like foxes, have dens of deceit,* and, since they have played the part of foxes, they shall have the portion of foxes.* As Solomon said, the same fate awaits man and beast.* Why should they not share the same fate, when they lived the same way? Man has occupied himself with earthly things, like beasts; he shall leave the earth like a beast. Again, is it strange that we should be allotted the same way of leaving life, when we shared the same way of entering it?* For it is only because of men's likeness to beasts that they have such ungovernable passion in copulation, and such excessive pain in giving

Ps 48:13

Ps 105:20
Mt 8:20

Ps 62:11
Qo 3:19

Wis 7:6

birth. Man, then, is comparable to foolish beasts* in copulation and birth, in life and death; and he has become like them.

6. Why is it that a free creature does not make himself master of his passions and rule them, but instead trails after them and is subject to them like a slave? Yet they are not called by nature to exercise freedom, but have been put under subjection to be slaves to their animal natures and obey their appetites. Surely God rises in wrath at being compared to such a creature, and considered like him! He said, 'You thought, wicked man, that I was like yourself',* and also, 'I will reprove you, and lay a charge against you'.* A soul which knows itself is not likely to imagine God to be like itself, particularly if it is a soul like mine, sinful and unrighteous. It is such a soul to which is uttered the reproof, 'You thought, wicked man'—he does not say, 'You thought, O soul', or 'you thought, O man, that I would be like you'. But if the wicked man is made to look at himself and to stand face to face with the deathly and decaying appearance of his inner self until he cannot disguise or disown the uncleanness of his conscience, but must, even against his will, see the foulness of his own sins and look upon the deformity of his vices, he will certainly not be able to think that God is like him; he will be in despair when he sees the great difference between them, and I think he will cry out, 'Lord, who is like you?'*—which was indeed said in recognition of that new but voluntary unlikeness. But the primal likeness remains, and this increases the soul's distress at the

Ps 48:13

Rom 16:18
Ps 49:21

Ps 34:10

unlikeness. How good the one is, how evil the other! And the nature of each is shown more clearly as they are seen side by side.

7. When the soul perceives this great disparity within itself, it is torn between hope and despair, and can only cry, 'Lord, who is like you?'* It is drawn towards despair by so great an evil, but it is recalled to hope by such great goodness. Thus it is that the more it is offended by the evil it sees in itself, the more ardently it is drawn to the good which it likewise sees in itself, and the more it desires to become its true self, simple and righteous, fearing God and turning from evil.* Why can it not turn from that which it could approach? Why can it not approach what it could turn away from? But I must insist that we can only dare to undertake either of these things by grace, not by nature, nor even by effort. It is wisdom which overcomes malice,* not effort or nature. There is no difficulty in finding grounds for hope: the soul must turn to the Word.* The great dignity of the soul's relationship with the Word, which I have been talking of for three days, is not without effect—and its enduring likeness bears witness to this relationship. The Spirit courteously admits into its fellowship one who is like him by nature. Certainly in the natural order like seeks like. This is the cry of one who seeks: 'Return, O Shunamite, return, that we may look upon you.'* He would not see her when she was unlike him, but when she is like him he will look upon her, and he will allow her to look upon him. 'We know that when he will appear we shall be like him, for we shall see

Ibid.

Job 1:1

Wis 7:30

Sg 7:10

Sg 6:12

him as he is.'* So think of the question,
'Lord, who is like you?'* in terms of difficulty, not of impossibility.

8. Or, if you prefer, it is a cry of admira-
tion. It is assuredly a thing most marvellous
and astonishing, that likeness which accom-
panies the vision of God, and is itself the
vision. I can only describe it as subsisting in
charity. This vision is charity, and the likeness
is charity. Who would not be amazed at the
charity of God in recalling someone who has
spurned him? How deserving of censure* is
the unrighteous man who was mentioned
earlier as appropriating to himself the likeness
of God, but who by choosing unrighteousness becomes incapable of loving either himself or God. You know the words, 'He who
loves iniquity hates his own soul'.* When the
iniquity which is in partly the cause of
unrighteousness is taken away, there will be a
oneness of spirit, a reciprocal vision, and
reciprocal love. When what is perfect comes,
what is partial will be done away with;* and
the love between them will be chaste and
consummated, full recognition, open vision,*
strong unity, indivisible fellowship and perfect likeness. Then the soul will know as it is
known* and love as it is loved, and the Bridegroom will rejoice over the Bride, knowing
and known, loving and loved,* Jesus Christ
Our Lord, who is God above all, blessed for
ever. Amen.*

Jn 3:2
Ps 34:10

Ps 49:21

Ps 10:6

1 Cor 13:10

1 Kgs 3:1

1 Cor 13:12

Is 62:5

Rom 9:5

SERMON EIGHTY-THREE

I. HOW THE SOUL CAN RETURN WITH
CONFIDENCE FROM THESE EVILS TO THE
WORD TO BE REFORMED AND CON-
FORMED TO IT. II. HOW THE AFFECT
OF LOVE IS MORE POWERFUL THAN
OTHER AFFECTS. III. HOW THE BRIDE-
GROOM LOVES FIRST AND LOVES MORE
STRONGLY, WHEREAS FOR THE BRIDE
IT IS ENOUGH TO LOVE WITH HER WHOLE
BEING.

I. 1. **D**URING THE LAST THREE days
I have spent the time allotted
me in showing the affinity between the Word and the soul. What was the
value of all that labor? Surely this: we have
seen how every soul—even if burdened with

2 Tim 3:6

sin,* enmeshed in vice, ensnared by the
allurements of pleasure, a captive in exile,

Ps 68:3

imprisoned in the body, caught in mud,*
fixed in mire, bound to its members, a slave
to care, distracted by business, afflicted with
sorrow, wandering and straying, filled with
anxious forebodings and uneasy suspicions, a

Ex 2:22

stranger in a hostile land,* and, according to
the Prophet, sharing the defilement of the
dead and counted with those who go down

Baruch 3:11

into hell*—every soul, I say, standing thus
under condemnation and without hope, has

180

the power to turn and find it can not only
breathe the fresh air of the hope of pardon
and mercy, but also dare to aspire to the
nuptials of the Word, not fearing to enter
into alliance with God or to bear the sweet
yoke of love* with the King of angels. Why   Mt 11:30
should it not venture with confidence into the
presence of him by whose image it sees itself
honored, and in whose likeness it knows
itself made glorious? Why should it fear a
majesty when its very origin gives it ground
for confidence? All it has to do is to take care
to preserve its natural purity by innocence of
life, or rather to study to beautify and
adorn with the brightness of its actions and
dispositions the glorious beauty which is its
birthright.

2. Why then does it not set to work?
There is a great natural gift within us, and if
it is not allowed full play the rest of our
nature will go to ruin, as though it were being
eaten away by the rust of decay. This would
be an insult to its Creator. This is why God,
its Creator, desires the divine glory and nobility to be always preserved in the soul, so that
it may have within itself that by which it may
always be admonished by the Word, either to
stay with him or to return to him if it has
strayed. It does not stray by changing its place
or by walking, but it strays—as is the nature of
a spiritual substance, in its affections, or rather
its defections,[1] and it degenerates and be-

---

1. *affectibus immo defectibus. Affectus* has been translated through-
out as *affection*. On this important, but in English difficult, term, see
Thomas X. Davis, appendix to *William of Saint Thierry: The Mirror of
Faith* (CF 15:93-5).

comes unlike itself when it becomes unlike
him in its depravity of life and manners; but
this unlikeness is not the destruction of its
nature but a defect, for natural goodness is
increased as much by comparison with itself
as it is spoiled by communication with evil.

Sg 7:10 So the soul returns and is converted* to
the Word to be reformed by him and conformed to him. In what way? In charity—for
he says, 'Be imitators of God, like dear children, and walk in love, as Christ also has
Eph 5:1 loved you.'*

3. Such conformity weds the soul to the
Word, for one who is like the Word by nature
shows himself like him too in the exercise of
his will, loving as she is loved. When she loves
perfectly, the soul is wedded to the Word.
What is lovelier than this conformity? What is
more desirable than charity, by whose operation, O soul, not content with a human
master, you approach the Word with confidence, cling to him with constancy, speak to
him as to a familiar friend, and refer to him in
every matter with an intellectual grasp pro-
portionate to the boldness of your desire?
Truly this is a spiritual contract, a holy
marriage. It is more than a contract, it is an
embrace: an embrace where identity of will
1 Cor 6:17 makes of two can spirit.* There need be no
fear that inequality of persons should impair
the conformity of will, because love is no
respecter of persons. It is from loving, not
revering, that love receives its name. Let
someone filled with horror or stupor or fear
or wonder be content with reverence; where
there is love all these are unimportant. Love is

sufficient for itself; when love is present it absorbs and conquers all other affections. Therefore it loves what it loves, and it knows nothing else. He who is justly honored, held in awe, and admired, prefers to be loved. He and the soul are Bridegroom and Bride. What other bond or compulsion do you look for between those who are betrothed, except to love and be loved?

II. This bond is stronger even than nature's firm bond between parents and children. 'For this', it says in the Gospel, 'a man will leave his father and his mother and cleave to his bride.'* You see how strong this feeling is *Mt 19:5* between bride and bridegroom—it is stronger not only than other affections, but even than itself.

4. Now the Bridegroom is not only loving; he is love. Is he honor too? Some maintain that he is, but I have not read it. I have read that God is love, but not that he is honor.* *1 Jn 4:16* It is not that God does not desire honor, for he says, 'If I am a father, where is my honor?'* *Mal 1:6* Here he speaks as a father, but if he declares himself to be a husband I think he would change the expression and say, 'If I am a bridegroom, where is my love?' For he had previously said, 'If I am the Lord, where is my fear?'* God then requires that he should be *Ibid.* feared as the Lord, honored as a father, and loved as a bridegroom. Which of these is highest or most lofty? Surely it is love. Without it fear brings pain,* and honor has no grace. *1 Jn 4:18* Fear is the lot of a slave, unless he is freed by love. Honor which is not inspired by love is not honor but flattery. Honor & glory belong

1 Tim 1:17

to God alone,* but God will receive neither if they are not sweetened with the honey of love. Love is sufficient for itself; it gives pleasure to itself, & for its own sake. It is its own merit & own reward. Love needs no cause beyond itself, nor does it demand fruits; it is its own purpose. I love because I love; I love that I may love. Love is a great reality, and if it returns to its beginning and goes back to its origin, seeking its source again, it will always draw afresh from it, and thereby flow freely. Love is the only one of the motions of the soul, of its senses and affections, in which the creature can respond to its Creator, even if not as an equal, and repay his favor in some similar way. For example, if God is angry with me, am I to be angry in return? No, indeed,

Job 26:11

but I shall tremble with fear* and ask pardon. So also, if he accuses me, I shall not accuse him in return, but rather justify him. Nor, if he judges me, shall I judge him, but I shall adore him; and in saving me he does not ask to be saved by me; nor does he who sets all men free, need to be set free by me. If he commands, I must obey, and not demand his service or obedience. Now you see how different love is, for when God loves, he desires nothing but to be loved, since he loves us for no other reason than to be loved, for he knows that those who love him are blessed in their very love.

5. Love is a great reality; but there are degrees to it. The bride stands at the highest. Children love their father, but they are thinking of their inheritance, and as long as they have any fear of losing it, they honor more

than they love the one from whom they expect to inherit. I suspect the love which seems to be founded on some hope of gain. It is weak, for if the hope is removed it may be extinguished, or at least diminished. It is not pure, as it desires some return. Pure love has no self-interest. Pure love does not gain strength through expectation, nor is it weakened by distrust. This is the love of the bride, for this is the bride— with all that means. Love is the being and the hope of a bride. She is full of it, and the bridegroom is contented with it. He asks nothing else, and she has nothing else to give. That is why he is the bridegroom and she the bride; this love is the property only of the couple. No-one else can share it, not even a son.

III. Thus it is to his sons that he cries, 'Where is my honor?'* He does not say, *Mal 1:6* 'Where is my love?', for he guards the Bride's prerogative. Then, too, a man is bidden to honor his father and his mother;* nothing is *Deut 5:16* said about love—not because children should not love their parents but because most children are inclined to honor their parents rather than love them. It is true that the king's honor loves judgment,* but the love of *Ps 98:4* a bridegroom—or rather of the Bridegroom who is love—asks only the exchange of love and trust. Let the Beloved love in return. How can the bride—and the bride of Love—do other than love? How can Love not be loved?

6. Rightly, then, does she renounce all other affections* and devote herself to love *affectionibus* alone, for it is in returning love that she has the power to respond to love. Although she

may pour out her whole self in love, what is that compared to the inexhaustible fountain of his love? The stream of love does not flow equally from her who loves and from him who is love, the soul and the Word, the Bride and the Bridegroom, the Creator and the creature—any more than a thirsty man can be compared to a fountain. Will the Bride's vow perish, then, because of this? Will the desire of her heart, her burning love, her affirmation of confidence, fail in their purpose because she has not the strength to keep pace with a giant, or rival honey in sweetness, the lamb in gentleness, or the lily in whiteness? Because she cannot equal the brightness of the sun, and the charity of him who is Charity?* No.

1 Jn 4:16

Although the creature loves less, being a lesser being, yet if it loves with its whole heart* nothing is lacking, for it has given all. Such love, as I have said, is marriage, for a soul cannot love like this and not be beloved; complete and perfect marriage consists in the exchange of love.* No-one can doubt that the soul is first loved, and loved more intensely, by the Word; for it is anticipated and surpassed in its love. Happy the soul who is permitted to be anticipated in blessedness so sweet!* Happy the soul who has been allowed to experience the embrace of such bliss! For it is nothing other than love, holy and chaste, full of sweetness and delight, love utterly serene and true, mutual and deep, which joins two beings, not in one flesh, but in one spirit, making them no longer two but one.* As Paul says: 'He who is united to God is one spirit with him.'* On this matter let us listen

Mt 22:37

Mt 18:16

Ps 20:4

Mt 19:5

1 Cor 6:17

to her who by his anointing* and by con-   *1 Jn 2:27*
stant familiarity has become our teacher above
all others. But perhaps we had better keep
this for the beginning of another sermon,
so that we may not compress important
matter into the closing paragraph of a sermon. If you agree, I will make an end before
I come to the end of the subject, so that
tomorrow we may come in good time, hun-
gry to taste the delights which are the rewards
of holiness, which the souls of the blessed
may enjoy with the Word and from the
Word, the Bridegroom, Jesus Christ Our
Lord, who is God above all, blessed for ever.
Amen.*   *Rom 9:5*

SERMON EIGHTY-FOUR

I. HOW GREAT A GOOD IT IS TO SEEK
GOD, AND HOW THE SOUL IS AWAKENED
AND THE WILL INSPIRED TO DO THIS.
II. OF THE SOUL WHO IS ABLE TO
SEARCH FOR GOD, AND WHAT IT MEANS
TO BE SOUGHT BY GOD; THAT THIS IS
NECESSARY FOR THE SOUL, BUT NOT
FOR THE WORD.

Sg 3:1

I. 1. 'NIGHTLONG in my little bed I sought him whom my soul loves.'* It is a great good to seek God; in my opinion the soul knows no greater blessing. It is the first of its gifts and the final stage in its progress. It is inferior to none, and it yields place to none. What could be superior to it, when nothing has a higher place? What could claim a higher place, when it is the consummation of all things? What virtue can be attributed to anyone who does not seek God? What boundary can be set for anyone who does seek him? The psalmist says: 'Seek his face always.'* Nor, I think, will a soul cease to seek him even when it has found him. It is not with steps of the feet that God is sought but with the heart's desire; and when the soul happily finds him its desire is not quenched but kindled. Does the consummation of joy bring about the

Ps 104:4

188

consuming of desire? Rather it is oil poured
upon the flames. So it is. Joy will be fulfilled,*   *Ps 15:11*
but there will be no end to desire, and there-
fore no end to the search. Think, if you can,
of this eagerness to see God as not caused by
his absence, for he is always present; and
think of the desire for God as without fear of
failure, for grace is abundantly present.

2. Now see why I have begun in this way.
Surely so that every soul among you who is
seeking God may know that she has been
forestalled, and that she was found before she
was sought. This will avoid distorting her
greatest good into a great evil; for this is what
we do when we receive favors from God and
treat his gifts as though they were ours by
right, and do not give glory to God.* Thus   *Lk 17:18*
those who appear great because of the favors
they have received are accounted as little
before God because they have not given him
thanks. But I am understating the case.* The   *1 Cor 7:28*
words I have used, 'great' and 'little', are
inadequate to express my meaning, and con-
fuse the issue. I will make myself clear.
I should have said 'good' and 'evil'. For if a
man who is very good takes the credit for his
goodness he becomes correspondingly evil.
For this is a very evil thing. If anyone says
'Far be it from me! I know that it is by the
grace of God I am what I am,'* and then is   *1 Cor 15:10*
careful to take a little of the glory for the
favor he has received, is he not a thief and a
robber?* Such a man will hear these words: *Jn 10:1*
'Out of your own mouth I judge you, wicked
servant.'* What is more wicked than for a   *Lk 19:22*
servant to usurp the glory due his master?

Sg 3:1

Job 7:7

Ps 77:39

Ps 118:176

Rom 7:18

3. 'In my little bed nightlong I sought him whom my soul loves'.* The soul seeks the Word, but has been first sought by the Word. Otherwise when she had gone away from the Word, or been cast out, she would not turn back to look upon the good* she had left unless she were sought by the Word. For if a soul is left to herself she is like a wandering spirit which does not return.* Listen to someone who was a fugitive and a wanderer: 'I have gone astray as a sheep that was lost. O seek your servant.'* O man, do you want to return? But if it is a matter of will, why do you ask for help? Why do you beg elsewhere for what you have within yourself in abundance? Clearly because one wills it, but cannot do it, and this is a spirit which wanders and does not return. He who has not the will is yet further away; if a soul desires to return and asks to be sought, I would not say that it was entirely dishonored and abandoned. Whence does it obtain this desire? If I am not mistaken, it is the result of the soul being already sought and visited, and that seeking has not been fruitless, because it has activated the will, without which there could be no return. But the soul is so feeble, and the return so difficult, that it is not enough to be sought only once. The soul may have the will, but the will cannot act unless it has some supporting power. Paul says, 'The will is in me, but I have no power to perform it.'* We quoted the psalmist; what does he go on to ask? Simply to be sought. He would not ask this if he had not already been sought. He also prays, 'O seek your

servant';* that is asking that the God who
had given him the will might also give him
the power to perform it, at his good will.*

4. I do not think, however, that this passage can refer to such a soul, which has not
yet received the next grace; it desires to approach him 'whom her soul loves',* but is
powerless to do so. How can you apply to it
the words which follow?—that is, that she
rises and goes about the city, and seeks her
beloved through the streets and squares*—if
she herself needs to be sought? Let her seek
him as she can, provided she remembers that
she was first sought, as she was first loved; and
it is because of this that she herself both
seeks and loves. Let us also pray, beloved,
that his mercies may speedily go before us,*
for our need is great. I do not say this of all,*
for I know that many of you walk in the love
with which Christ has loved us,* and seek
him in simplicity of heart.*But there are some,
I am sad to say, who have not yet shown any
sign of this saving and prevenient grace, and
therefore no sign of salvation, men who love
themselves,* not the Lord, and are concerned
with their own interests, not his.*

5. 'I sought him whom my soul loves'*—
this is what you are urged to do by the goodness of him who anticipates you, who sought
him, and loved you before you loved him.*
You would not seek him or love him unless
you had first been sought and loved. Not
only in one blessing* have you been forestalled but in two, being loved as well as being
sought. For the love is the reason for the
search, and the search is the fruit of the love,

Ps 118:176

Ph 2:13

Sg 3:1

Sg 3:2

Ps 78:8
Jn 13:18

Eph 5:2
Wis 1:1

2 Tim 3:2
1 Cor 13:5

Sg 3:1

1 Jn 4:10

Gen 27:28

and its certain proof. You are loved so that you may not suppose you are sought to be punished. You are sought so that you may not complain you are loved in vain. Both these loving and manifest favors give you courage, and drive away your diffidence, persuading you to return, and stirring your affections.* From this comes the zeal and ardor to seek him whom your soul loves,* because you cannot seek unless you are sought, and when you are sought you cannot but seek.

6. Do not forget whence you came. Now, that I may take the words to myself*—which is the safest course—is it not you, my soul, who left your first husband,* with whom it went well with you, and cast aside your loyalty* by going after lovers?† And now that you have chosen to commit fornication with them and have been cast aside by them, do you have the effrontery, the insolence, to return to him whom you spurned in your arrogance? Do you seek the light when you are only fit to be hidden, and run to the Bridegroom when you are more deserving of blows than of embraces? It will be a wonder if you do not meet the judge rather than the bridegroom. Happy the person who hears his soul replying to these reproaches, 'I do not fear, because I love; and I could not love at all if I were not loved; therefore this is love.' One who is loved has nothing to fear. Let those fear who do not love; they must always live in fear of retribution. Since I love, I cannot doubt that I am loved, any more than I can doubt that I love. Nor can I fear to look

Margin notes:

affectus
Sg 3:1

1 Cor 4:6

Si 23:32

*1 Tim 5:12
†Hos 2:5, 13

on his face, since I have sensed his tenderness.* In what have I known it? In this—not
only has he sought me as I am, but he has shown
me tenderness,* and caused me to seek him
with confidence. How can I not respond to him
when he seeks me, since I respond to him in
tenderness?* How can he be angry with me for
seeking him, when he overlooked the contempt
I showed for him? He will not drive away someone who seeks him, when he sought someone
who spurned him. The spirit of the Word is
gentle,* and brings me gentle greetings, speaking to me persuasively of the zeal and desire of
the Word, which cannot be hidden from him.*
He searches the deep things of God,* and
knows his thoughts—thoughts of peace & not
of vengeance.* How can I fail to be inspired to
seek him, when I have experienced his mercy
and been assured of his peace?

7. Brothers, to realize this is to be taught
by the Word; to be convinced of it is to be
found. But not everyone can receive this
word.* What shall we do for our little ones,
those among us who are beginners—not foolish,* since they have the beginning of wis-
dom† and are subject to one another in the
fear of Christ?* How can we make them
believe that it is the Bridegroom who deals
thus with them, when they themselves cannot
yet perceive what is happening to them? But
I send them to one whom they should not
disbelieve. Let them read in the book what
they do not see in the heart of another, and
therefore do not believe. It is written in the
prophets, 'If a man puts away his wife and
she goes away and takes another husband,

sensui affectum

affecit

in affectu

Wis 1:6

Mt 5:14
1 Cor 2:10

Jer 29:11

Mt 19:11

incipientes non
insipientes
†*Ps 110:10*
Eph 5:21

Jer 3:1

will he return to her? Will that woman not be dishonored and disgraced? But you have committed fornication with many lovers; yet return to me, says the Lord, and I will take you back.* These are the words of the Lord; you cannot refuse to believe them. What they do not know from experience, let them believe, so that one day, by virtue of their faith, they may reap the harvest of experience.

I think enough has been explained of what is meant by being sought by the Word, and that this is necessary, not for the Word but for the soul. We must however add that the soul which knows this by experience has fuller and more blessed knowledge. It remains for me to show in my next sermon how thirsty souls seek him by whom they are sought; or rather we should learn it from the one who is mentioned in this passage as seeking him whom her soul loves,* the Bridegroom of the soul, Jesus Christ our Lord, who is God above all, blessed for ever. Amen.*

Sg 3:3

Rom 9:5

SERMON EIGHTY-FIVE

I. SEVEN REASONS WHY THE SOUL
SEEKS THE WORD; FIRST, CONCERNING
CORRECTION AND RECOGNITION.
II. THAT THE SOUL SUFFERS A THREE-
FOLD ATTACK, AND HOW MAN MUST
GUARD AGAINST THIS; OF THE NATURE
OF VIRTUE, AND HOW HE WHO TRUSTS
IN CHRIST IS ALL-POWERFUL, FOR IT IS
CHRIST WHO MUST BE RELIED UPON IN
PURSUIT OF VIRTUE. III. HOW WE ARE
CONFORMED AFRESH TO VIRTUE BY THE
WORD, AND THE DIFFERENCE BETWEEN
WISDOM AND VIRTUE. IV. WHAT IT
MEANS TO BE CONFORMED TO THE
WORD IN BEAUTY; OF THE FRUITFUL-
NESS OF MARRIAGE, AND ITS ENJOY-
MENT, AS FAR AS POSSIBLE, IN THIS
LIFE.

I. 1. 'IN MY LITTLE BED I sought him whom my soul loves.'* For what? I have already spoken of that, and it is redundant to repeat it. But for the sake of some who were not present when it was discussed, I will give a short account, and perhaps those who were present will not object to listening; for it could not be treated fully on that occasion. The soul seeks the Word, and consents to receive correction, by which

Sg 3:1

she may be enlightened to recognize him,
strengthened to attain virtue, moulded to wisdom, conformed to his likeness, made fruitful
by him, and enjoy him in bliss. These are the
reasons why the soul seeks the Word. No doubt
there are countless others, but these occur to
me at the moment. If anyone has a mind to do
so, he can easily find many others in himself;
for we experience many vicissitudes, many
deep spiritual needs, and unnumbered anxieties.* But the word is so fully, so richly endowed with goodness that his Wisdom overcomes our malice,* vanquishing evil with good.†
Now I will give you the reasoning behind my
statement. See first how the soul consents to
receive correction. We read in the Gospel how
the Word says, 'Agree with your adversary
quickly, while you are in the way with him, so
that he does not hand you over to the judge,
& the judge to the executioner.'* What better
counsel could there be? It is the counsel of the
Word, who is himself the adversary of our carnal desires,* when he says, 'These people always
err in their hearts.'* If you who are listening
to me have conceived a wish to flee from the
wrath to come,* you will, I think, be anxious
to know how you are to agree with this adversary* who seems to threaten you so terribly.
This will be impossible unless you disagree
with yourself & become your own adversary,
and fight against yourself without respite in a
continual and hard struggle, and renounce
your inveterate habits and inborn inclinations.
But this is a hard thing. If you attempt it in
your own strength, it will be as though you
were trying to stop the raging of a torrent, or

Ps 39:13

*Wis 7:30
†Rom 12:21

Cf. Mt 5:25

1 Pet 2:11
Ps 94:10

Lk 3:7

Mt 5:25

to make the Jordan run backwards.* What
can you do then? You must seek the Word, to
agree with him, by his operation. Flee to him
who is your adversary, that through him you
may no longer be his adversary, but that he
who threatens you may caress you and may
transform you by his outpoured grace more
effectually than by his outraged anger.

2. This, I think, is the first and most urgent compulsion which drives the soul to seek
the Word. But if you do not know what he
wills with whom you have reached agreement
of will, shall he not say of you that you have a
zeal for God, but it is not knowledgeable?*
And if you think this unimportant, remember
that it is written, 'he who does not know will
not be known'.* Do you want to know what
advice I would give in this difficulty? First of
all, my advice is that you go now to the Word,
and he will teach you his ways,* so that you
will not go astray in your journey and, desiring the good but not recognizing it, wander in
a pathless place* instead of along the high-
way. The Word is the light.* 'The unfolding
of your words gives light and imparts understanding to children.'* Happy are you if you
too can say, 'Your word is a lamp for my feet
and a lantern for my path'.* Your soul has
received great profit if your will is unswerving
and your reason enlightened, willing and recognizing the good. By the first it receives life
and by the second vision; for it was dead when
it desired evil, and blind when it did not
recognize the good.

3. But now it lives and sees, and stands
firm in the good—but by the operation and

Ps 113:3

Rom 10:2

1 Cor 14:38

Ps 24:9

Ps 106:40
Jn 1:9

Ps 118:130

Ps 118:105

with the help of the Word. Raised by the hand
of the Word it stands, as it were, on the two
feet of devotion and knowledge. It stands, I
say; but let it take to itself the saying, 'Let
him who thinks he stands take heed lest he

1 Cor 10:12
fall'.* Do you imagine he can stand in his own
strength, when he could not rise in his own
strength? How could he? 'The heavens were

Ps 32:6
established by the word of the Lord'*—can
the earth stand without the Word? If it were
able to stand in its own strength, why did a
man, also of the earth, pray, 'Strengthen me

Ps 118:28
according to your word'?* Surely he spoke
from experience. It was his voice which said,
'I was attacked and thrown down and would

Ps 117:13
have fallen, but the Lord sustained me'.*

II.   Who was it who attacked him? It was not
only one. The devil attacked him, the world
attacked him, a man attacked him. What
man? Every man is his own attacker. Every
man throws himself down—indeed you need
not fear any attack from outside, if you can
keep your hands from yourself. 'For who can
harm you', says the Apostle, 'if you follow

1 Pet 3:13
what is good?'* By your hand I mean the
consent of your will. If the devil suggests you
should do wrong, or the pressure of the
world prompts you, and you withhold your
consent and do not allow your limbs to be

Rom 6:13
instruments of iniquity* nor permit sin to
Rom 6:12
control your mortal body,* you have proved
that you follow what is good, and the malice
of the attack has done you no harm, but has
instead benefitted you. For it is written, 'Do

Rom 13:3
good, and you shall receive praise for it'.*

Those who tried to attack your soul have
been routed, and you can sing, 'If they have
no dominion over me, then shall I be blameless'.* You have shown clearly that you fol- *Ps 39:15*
low what is good,* if, following the wise man's *Ps 18:14*
advice, you love your own soul,* guard your *Si 30:24*
heart with all vigilance,* and keep yourself *Prov 4:23*
pure,* as the Apostle enjoins. If you do not, *1 Tim 5:22*
even if you gain the whole world, but let
your soul go to ruin* we cannot consider you *Mt 16:26*
as following what is good; for the Saviour
himself will not do so.

4. There are three agents, then, who
always constitute a threat: the devil, who
attacks with envy and malice; the world,
with the blasting wind of vanity; and man, by
the burden of his own corruption. The devil
attacks, but he does not overthrow you if you
refuse to help him or to give your consent.
You know the saying, 'Resist the devil, and
he will flee from you.'* For it was he who in *Jas 4:7*
envy attacked the denizens of paradise and
overthrew them, but they gave their consent
and put up no resistance. It was he who fell
from heaven in his pride; no-one attacked
him. You can see how much more danger
there is that a man will precipitate his own
fall, since he is weighed down by his own
material being.

Then there is the attack from the world,
which is rooted in wickedness.* The world *1 Jn 5:19*
attacks everyone, but it only overthrows
those who are its friends and acquiesce with
it. I have no wish to be a friend to the world
and court the danger of falling. 'He who
desires to be a friend of this world makes

himself the enemy of God',* and there can be no worse fall than that. So it is quite clear that man is his own greatest threat, for he can fall by his own momentum without any impulse from anyone else, but not without an impulse of his own. Which of these needs to be resisted most? The last, for it is nearest to us, and therefore more troublesome, being enough in itself to cast us down, whereas without it no-one else can harm us.*

Jn 15:5

It is not without reason that the Wise Man accounted the man who has command of his spirit greater than he who storms a city.* This is very important for you: you have need of strength, and not simply strength, but strength drawn from above.* For this strength, if it is perfect, will easily give the mind* control of itself, and so it will be unconquered before all its adversaries. It is a strength of mind which, in protecting reason, does not know how to retreat. Or, if you like, it is the strength of a mind standing steadfast with reason and for reason. Or again, it is a strength of mind which gathers up and directs everything towards reason.

Prov 16:32

Lk 24:49

animus, throughout. Cf. ¶ 8, 13.

Ps 23:3

5. 'Who shall ascend the hill of the Lord?'* If anyone aspires to climb to the summit of that mountain,* that is to the perfection of virtue, he will know how hard the climb is, and how the attempt is doomed to failure without the help of the Word. Happy the soul which causes the angels to look at her with joy and wonder and hears them saying, 'Who is this coming up from the wilderness, rich in grace and beauty, leaning upon her beloved?'* Otherwise, unless it leans on him, its struggle

Ex 24:17

Sg 8:5

is in vain. But it will gain force by struggling with itself and, becoming stronger, will impel all things towards reason: anger, fear, covetousness, and joy; like a good charioteer, it will control the chariot of the mind, bringing every carnal affect into captivity,* and every *2 Cor 10:5* sense under the control of reason in accordance with virtue. Surely all things are possible to someone who leans upon him who can do all things? What confidence there is in the cry, 'I can do all things in him who strengthens me!'* Nothing shows more clearly *Ph 4:13* the almighty power of the Word than that he makes all-powerful all those who put their hope in him. For 'all things are possible to one who believes'.* If all things are possible to him *Mk 9:22* he must be all-powerful.* Thus if the mind *Mt 19:26* does not rely upon itself, but is strengthened by the Word, it can gain such command over itself that no unrighteousness will have power over it.* So, I say, neither power, nor *Ps 118:133* treachery, nor lure, can overthrow or hold in subjection the mind which rests upon the Word and is clothed with strength from above.* *Lk 24:49*

6. Do you wish to be free from fear of attack? Let the foot of pride not come near you, then the hand of an attacker shall not move you.* 'There lie those who work *Ps 35:12* wickedness.'* There fell the devil and his *Ps 35:13* angels, who were not attacked from without, yet could not stand and were driven out. So he who did not rest on the Word but relied on his own strength* did not stand in the *Jn 8:44* truth.* Perhaps that is why he wished to sit, *Ps 48:7* because he had not the strength to stand; for

Is 14:13

Lk 10:18
1 Cor 10:12

Jn 15:5

Cf. Jn 9:24

Ps 39:3
Acts 9:41

1 Cor 1:24

*Jas 1:5
†1 Tim 1:25

cognata sapientiae

he said, 'I will sit on the mountain of assembly'.* But the judgement of God was otherwise: he neither stood nor sat, but fell, as the Lord said, 'I beheld Satan fallen like lightning from heaven'.* Therefore anyone who stands* and does not wish to fall, should not place his trust in himself, but lean on the Word. The Word says, 'without me you can do nothing'.* And so it is. We can neither rise to the good nor stand in the good without the Word. Therefore, you who stand, give glory to the Word* and say, 'He set my feet upon a rock, and directed my path aright.'* You must be held by the strength of him by whose hand you were raised.* This is to explain what I meant when I said that we had need of the Word on whom to lean in our pursuit of virtue.

III. 7. Now we must consider my other words, that we are conformed to wisdom by the Word. The Word is strength and he is wisdom.* Let the soul therefore draw strength from his strength and wisdom from his wisdom; let it ascribe both gifts to the Word alone. For if she ascribes either to another source, or claims the credit for herself, she might as well say that the river does not come from the spring, nor the wine from the grape, nor light from light. 'If anyone has need of wisdom, let him ask it from God, who gives to all freely and utters no reproach, and he will give it to him.* A faithful saying.† I think the same applies to virtue, for virtue is the sister of wisdom.* Virtue is God's gift and must be counted among his best gifts,

coming down from the Father of the Word.* *Jas 1:17, 3:15*
If anyone thinks that wisdom is the same in
all respects,* I do not dissent, but this holds *Gal 6:3*
good in the Word, not in the soul. For the
attributes which are in the Word, because
of the singular simplicity of the divine nature,
do not have a single action on the soul, but
are applied to its various different needs as
though they were different and could be
divided. It follows this reasoning that to be
moved by virtue* is one thing and to be ruled *Ps 65:7*
by wisdom another; it is one thing to be
controlled in virtue, and another to be delighted by sweetness. For although wisdom is
powerful and virtue sweet, if we are to give
words their proper significance, virtue is
characterized by strength of mind, and wisdom by peace of mind and spiritual sweet-
ness.* This I think was what the Apostle *Cf. Si, Prol.*
meant when, after a long exhortation to
virtue, he mentions what wisdom there is in
sweetness, in the Holy Spirit.* It is an honor, *2 Cor 6:6*
therefore, to stand firm, to resist, to meet
force with force—these are considered works
of virtue—but it is hard work. For defending
your honor with toil is not the same as pos-
sessing it in peace. Nor is being moved by
virtue the same as enjoying virtue. What virtue wins by toil, wisdom enjoys; and what is
ordained, counselled, and guided by wisdom
is accomplished by virtue.

8. 'The wisdom of a scribe comes by
leisure', says Solomon.* Therefore the leisure *Si 38:25*
of wisdom is exertion,* and the more leisure sapientiae otia
negotia sunt.
wisdom has, the harder it works in its own
fashion. But the more virtue is exercised in its

own sphere, the more illustrious it is, and the more ready it is to serve, the more approval it wins, If anyone defines wisdom as the love of virtue, I think you are not far from the truth. For where there is love, there is no toil, but a taste. Perhaps *sapientia,* that is wisdom, is derived from *sapor,* that is taste, because, when it is added to virtue, like some seasoning, it adds taste to something which by itself is tasteless and bitter. I think it would be permissible to define wisdom as a taste for goodness. We lost this taste almost from the creation of our human race. When the old serpent's poison infected the palate of our heart, because the fleshly sense prevailed, the soul began to lose its taste for goodness, and a depraved taste crept in. 'A man's imagination and thoughts are evil from his youth',* that is, as a result of the folly of the first woman. So it was folly which drove the taste for good from the woman, because the serpent's malice outwitted the woman's folly. But the reason which caused the malice to appear for a time victorious, is the same reason why it suffers eternal defeat. For see! It is again the heart and body of a woman which wisdom fills and makes fruitful so that, as by a woman we were deformed into folly, so by a woman we may be reformed to wisdom. Now wisdom always prevails over malice* in the minds† which it has entered, and drives out the taste for evil which the other has brought to it, by introducing something better. When wisdom enters, it makes the carnal sense taste flat, it purifies the understanding, cleanses and heals the palate of the heart. Thus, when the palate

Gen 18:21 (margin)

*Wis 7:30 (margin)
†mentes (margin)

is clean, it tastes the good, it tastes wisdom
itself, and there is nothing better.

9. How many good actions are performed
without the doers having any taste for them,
because they are compelled to do them by
their way of life or by some circumstance or
necessity? And on the contrary many who
do evil with no taste for it are led by fear or
desire for something, rather than because they
relish evil. But those who act in accordance
with the affection of their hearts* are either *Ps 72:7*
wise, and delight in goodness because they
have a taste for it, or else they are wicked, and
take pleasure in wrong-doing, even if they are
not moved by any hope of gain. For what is
malice but a taste for evil? Happy is the mind
which is protected by a taste for good and a
hatred of evil, for this is what it means to be
reformed to wisdom, and to know by experience and to rejoice in the victory of wisdom. For in nothing is the victory of wisdom
over malice* more evident than when the *Wis 7:30*
taste for evil—which is what malice is—is
purged away, and the mind's inmost task
senses that it is deeply filled with sweetness.
It looks to virtue to sustain tribulations with
fortitude, and to wisdom to rejoice in those
tribulations.* To strengthen your heart and *2 Cor 7:4*
to wait upon the Lord—that is virtue;* to *Ps 26:14*
taste and see that the Lord is good—that is
wisdom.* Now both goods are best seen as *Ps 33:9*
arising from their appropriate nature. Thus
modesty of mind* marks the man who is *animus*
wise, and constancy the man of virtue. It is
right to put wisdom after virtue, for virtue
is, as it were, the sure foundation* above *Prov 9:1*

which wisdom builds her home. But the
knowledge of good should come before these,
because there is no fellowship between the
light of wisdom and the shadows of ignorance.*
Goodwill, too, should come before them,
because wisdom will not enter a soul disposed
to ill.*

IV. 10. Now the soul has recovered its life
by changing its will, its health by instruction,
its stability by virtue, and its maturity by
wisdom. It remains for us to find how to obtain the beauty without which it cannot please
him who is lovelier than all the sons of men.*
For it hears that 'the king shall desire your
beauty'.* What great spiritual goods we have
mentioned: gifts from the Word, goodwill,
knowledge, virtue, wisdom! Yet we read that
none of them is desired by the king, who is
the Word, but it only says, 'the king shall
desire your beauty'.* The prophet says, 'The
Lord is king, he is clothed in beauty'. How
can he but desire a like garment for his Bride,
who is also his likeness? And the closer the
likeness, the dearer she will be to him. What
is this spiritual beauty? Does it consist of
what we call honor? Let us take it as such
for the moment, until we find something
better. But honor concerns outward behavior
—not that honor issues from it, but is perceived through it. Its root and its dwelling are
in the conscience; and the evidence of a good
conscience is its clarity. There is nothing
clearer than this transparent goodness, which
is the light of truth shining in the mind; there
is nothing more glorious than the mind which

2 Cor 6:14

Wis 1:4

Ps 44:3

Ps 44:12

Ps 92:1

sees itself in the truth. But what is this mind
like? It is modest, reverent, filled with holy
fear, watchful, guarding against anything
which might dim the glory of its conscience,*   *Cf. 2 Cor 3:7*
aware of nothing which might make it
ashamed in the presence of the truth or
cause it to avert its gaze from the light of
God in confusion and terror. This is the glory
which delights the eyes of God above all
qualities of the soul,* and this is what we   *Cf. Mt 24:47*
mean by honor.

11. But when this beauty and brightness
has filled the inmost part of the heart, it must
become outwardly visible, and not be like
a lamp hidden under a bushel,* but be a light   *Mt 5:15*
shining in darkness,* which cannot be hidden.   *Jn 1:5*
It shines out, and by the brightness of its rays
it makes the body a mirror of the mind,
spreading through the limbs and senses so that
every action, every word, look, movement and
even laugh (if there should be laughter)
radiates gravity and honor. So when the
movements of the limbs and senses, its
gestures and habits, are seen to be resolute,
pure, restrained, free from all presumption
and licence, with no sign of triviality and idle-
ness, but given to just dealing, zealous in
piety, then the beauty of the soul will be
seen openly—that is, if there is no guilt in the
spirit,* for these qualities can be counter-   *Ps 31:2*
feited, and not spring from the heart's abundance.* Now let us elucidate what we mean   *Mt 12:34*
by honor, and wherein it may be found; so
that the soul's beauty may shine forth even
more. It is integrity of mind, which is concerned to keep the innocent reputation with a

1 Tim 1:5

2 Cor 8:21

good conscience,* and not only, as the Apostle says, to provide things good in the sight of God,* but in the sight of men also. Happy the mind which has clothed itself in the beauty of holiness and the brightness of innocence, by which it manifests its glorious likeness, not to the world but to the Word, of of whom we read that he is the brightness of eternal life,* the splendor and image of the being of God.*

Wis 7:26

Heb 1:3

12. The soul which has attained this degree now ventures to think of marriage. Why should she not, when she sees that she is like him and therefore ready for marriage? His loftiness has no terrors for her, because her likeness to him associates her with him, and her declaration of love is a betrothal. This is the form of that declaration: 'I have sworn and I purpose to keep your righteous judgements.'* The apostles followed this when they said, 'See, we have left everything to follow you'.* There is a similar saying which pointing to the spiritual marriage between Christ and the Church, refers to physical marriage: 'For this shall a man leave his father and mother and be joined to his wife, and they two shall be one flesh';* and the prophet says of the Bride's glory: 'It is good to me to cling to good, and to put my hope in the Lord.'* When you see a soul leaving everything* and clinging to the Word with all her will and desire, living for the Word, ruling her life by the Word, conceiving by the Word what it will bring forth by him, so that she can say, 'For me to live is Christ, and to die is gain',* you know that the soul is the spouse and

Ps 118:106

Mt 19:27

Eph 5:31

Ps 72:28

Lk 5:11

Ph 1:21

bride of the Word. The heart of the Bride-
groom has faith* in her, knowing her to be   *Prov 31:11*
faithful, for she has rejected all things as
dross to gain him.* He knows her to be like   *Ph 3:8*
him of whom it was said, 'He is a chosen vessel for me.'* Paul's soul indeed was like a   *Acts 9:15*
tender mother and a faithful wife when he
said, 'My little children, with whom I travail
in birth again, until Christ shall be formed
in you.'*   *Gal 4:11*

13. But notice that in spiritual marriage
there are two kinds of birth, and thus two
kinds of offspring, though not opposite. For
spiritual persons, like holy mothers, may
bring souls to birth by preaching, or may give
birth to spiritual insights by meditation. In
this latter kind of birth the soul leaves even
its bodily senses and is separated from them,
so that in her awareness of the Word she is
not aware of herself. This happens when the
mind* is enraptured by the unutterable sweet-   mens
ness of the Word, so that it withdraws, or
rather is transported, and escapes from itself
to enjoy the Word. The soul is affected in one
way when it is made fruitful by the Word, in
another when it enjoys the Word: in the one
it is considering the needs of its neighbor; in
the other it is allured by the sweetness of the
Word. A mother is happy in her child; a bride
is even happier in her bridegroom's embrace.
The children are dear, they are pledge of his
love, but his kisses give her greater pleasure.
It is good to save many souls, but there is
far more pleasure in going aside to be with
the Word.* But when does this happen, and   *2 Cor 5:13*
for how long? It is sweet intercourse, but

lasts a short time and is experienced rarely! This is what I spoke of before, when I said that the final reason for the soul to seek the Word was to enjoy him in bliss.

14. There may be someone who will go on to ask me, 'What does it mean to enjoy the Word?' I would answer that he must find someone who has experience of it, and ask him. Do you suppose, if I were granted that experience, that I could describe to you what is beyond description? Listen to one who has known it: 'If we are beside ourselves, it is for God; if we are in our right mind, it is for *2 Cor 5:13* you.'* That is to say, it is one thing for me to be with God, and of that, God alone is the judge. It is another for me to be with you. I may have been granted this experience, but I do not speak of it. I have made allowance in what I have said, so that you could understand me. Oh, whoever is curious to know what it means to enjoy the Word, make ready your mind, not your ear! The tongue does not teach this, grace does. It is hidden from the wise and prudent, and revealed to chil-*Lk 10:21* dren.* Humility, my brothers, is a great virtue, great and sublime. It can attain to what it cannot learn; it is counted worthy to possess what it has not the power to possess; it is worthy to conceive by the Word and from the Word what it cannot itself explain in words. Why is this? Not because it deserves to do so, but because it pleases the Father of the *Cf. 1 Jn 3:22* Word,* the Bridegroom of the soul, Jesus Christ our Lord, who is God above all, *Rom 9:5* blessed for ever. Amen.*

SERMON EIGHTY-SIX

I. IN PRAISE OF THE MODESTY OF THE
BRIDE, AND HOW THIS IS FITTING FOR
THE YOUNG. II. OF THE PLACE AND
TIME SUITABLE FOR PRAYER, AND WHAT
CAN BE RIGHTLY UNDERSTOOD BY THE
BED AND THE NIGHT.

I. 1. THERE IS NO REASON to ask me further why the soul should seek the Word; I have said more than enough. Let us now continue our consideration of the rest of this passage, insofar as it refers to conduct of life. First then observe the modesty of the Bride; surely nothing in human conduct can be counted lovelier. This is what I should like above all to take in my hands and pluck, like a beautiful flower, to present to all our young people—not that it should not be held with the greatest care by everyone who is older, for the grace of modesty is an adornment to persons of all ages, but because, being tender, it shines out with greater brightness and beauty in those of tender age. What is more endearing in a young man than modesty? How lovely it is, and what a bright jewel in the life and bearing of a young man! What a true and sure indication of hope it is, the mark of a good disposition! It is the rod of discipline,* chastening the   *Prov 22:15*

211

affections and controlling the thoughtless actions and impulses of an age which lacks stability, and checking its arrogance. What is so far removed from evil-speaking or any kind of bad behaviour? It is the sister of self-control. There is no clearer indication of dove-like simplicity,* and thus it is the mark of innocence. It is the lamp which lights the unassuming mind,* so that nothing dishonorable or unbecoming may attempt to dwell in it without being instantly discovered. Thus it is the destroyer of evils and the protector of its inborn purity, the particular glory of the conscience, the guardian of its reputation, the adornment of its life, the seat of virtue and its firstfruits, the boast of nature and the mark of all honor. Even the blush which modesty brings to the cheeks gives grace and beauty to the countenance.

2. Modesty is a quality so natural to the mind* that even those who do not fear to do wrong are reluctant to let it be seen. The Lord said, 'Every man who does evil hates the light',* and also, 'those who sleep sleep at night, and those who are drunk are drunk at night';* the works of darkness which should be hidden conceal themselves in darkness. There is a difference, however, between the modesty of those who do not hesitate to commit deeds of wickedness, but are reluctant to reveal them, and that of the Bride who has no dealings with them, but rejects them and drives them away. Therefore Solomon says, 'There is a shame which brings sin, and there is a shame which is glory and grace.'* The Bride seeks the Word with

Mt 10:16

mens

animus

Jn 3:20

1 Th 5:7

Si 4:25

modesty, in her bed, at night; but this modesty brings glory, not sin. She seeks him to purify her conscience, she seeks him to obtain a testimony, so that she can say, 'This is my glory, the testimony of my conscience.* In my little bed nightlong I sought him whom my soul loves.'* Her modesty, you observe, is indicated both by the place and the time. What is more welcome to a modest mind than privacy? Night and her bed insures her privacy. Now when we wish to pray, we are bidden to enter our room,* for the sake of privacy. This is a precaution, for if we pray when others are present, their approbation may rob our prayer of its fruit and nullify its effect. But from this injunction you may also learn modesty. What is more appropriate to modesty than the avoidance of praise or ostentation? It is clear that the Son, our teacher, has enjoined us to seek privacy when we pray, in order to promote modesty. What is so unseemly, particularly in a young man, as showing-off holiness? It is at this age that the elements of religious obedience can be best learned. Jeremiah said, 'It is good for a man to bear the yoke in his youth'.* It is to be recommended that when you go to pray you first mention your modesty and say, 'I am small and of no importance; yet I do not forget your precepts.'*

3. Anyone who wishes to pray must choose not only the right place but also the right time. A time of leisure is best and most convenient, the deep silence when others are asleep is particularly suitable, for prayer will then be freer and purer. 'Arise at the first

2 Cor 1:12

Sg 3:1

Mt 6:6

Lam 3:27

Ps 118:141

Lam 2:19

watch of the night, and pour out your heart like water before the face of the Lord, your God.'* How secretly prayer goes up in the night, witnessed only by God and the holy angel who received it to present it at the heavenly altar! How pleasing, how unclouded it is, colored with the blush of modesty! How serene, how calm, free from noise and interruption! How pure it is, how sincere, unsullied by the dust of earthly care, untouched by ostentation or human flattery! Therefore the Bride, as modest as she is cautious, when she desired to pray, that is, to seek the Word—for they are the same—sought the privacy of her bed at night. You will not pray aright, if in your prayers you seek anything but the Word, or seek him for the sake of anything but the Word; for in him are all things.* In him is healing for your wounds, help in your need, restoration for your faults, resources for your further growth; in him is all that men should ask or desire, all they need, all that will profit them. There is no reason therefore to ask anything else of the Word, for he is all. Even if we seem sometimes to ask for material things, providing that we do so for the sake of the Word, as we should, it is not the things themselves that we are asking for, but him for whose sake we ask them. Those who habitually use all things to find the Word know this.

Col 1:17

4. It will repay us to examine further the privacy of the bed and the time, to see if there is any hidden spiritual meaning which it will be to our advantage to reveal. If we take the bed to mean human weakness, and the dark-

ness of night human ignorance, it follows
logically that the Bride is seeking the Word,
the power of God & the wisdom of God,* to   *1 Cor 1:24*
overcome these two ills: power to streng-
then her weakness and wisdom to enlighten
her ignorance. Nothing could be more fitting.
But if any lingering doubt about this interpretation remains in the hearts of the simple,
let them hear what the holy prophet says on
this matter: 'The Lord strengthens him on his
bed of sickness; it is you who make his bed in
his weakness.'* This is enough about the bed.   *Ps 40:4*
Now as regards the night of ignorance, what
could be clearer than what is said in another
psalm: 'They have not known, they have not
understood, they walk in darkness.'* Does   *Ps 81:5*
this not express perfectly the ignorance in
which the whole human race was born? This
is the ignorance, I think, which the blessed
Apostle admits he was born in, and gives
thanks that he was rescued from, when he
says, 'He has snatched us from the power of
darkness'.* Again, he says to all the elect, 'We   *Col 1:13*
are not children of the night or of darkness;*   *1 Th 5:5*
walk as children of the light.'*   *Eph 5:8*

*Bernard of Clairvaux died in 1153, without
completing his sermon commentaries on the
Song of Songs. The work was taken up by
John, Abbot of Ford and then by Gilbert of
Hoyland, abbot of Swineshead Abbey in Eng-
land, who had, perhaps, been a monk at
Clairvaux, while Bernard was abbot.*

A Cumulative Index to Bernard of Clairvaux's

SERMONS ON THE SONG OF SONGS

SCRIPTURAL INDEX

Column one indicates the scriptural book and its abbreviations. Column two indicates the bernardine sermon and its paragraph. Roman numerals within the sermons have not been indicated.

Genesis *(Gen, Gn)*

1:1	67:5
1:4	33:13; 71:1
1:7	75:8
1:26	21:6; 24:5; 25:7; 53:8; 68:2; 77:5
1:27	18:6; 66:4; 80:2; 81:1
2:6	54:6
2:7	16:2; 72:7
2:8	35:3
2:9	48:5
2:18	24:6
2:19	82:4
2:23	2:6
2:24	7:2; 8:9; 27:7
2:26	71:7
3:1-5	82:3
3:5	69:2
3:6	72:7; 82:4
3:7	72:7
3:8	82:4
3:9	28:7
3:12	16:11
3:18	30:7; 48:1; 58:7; 70:5,8
3:19	9:2; 53:5; 78:2
3:21	28:2
3:22	35:3; 54:1 59:2; 72:7
4:4-5	71:3
4:5	24:7; 71:13
4:7	24:7
4:8	24:7
4:10	16:5; 66:9
4:13	11:2; 16:12; 61:4
5:2	80:2
5:3	81:1
7:1	38:4
7:11	26:8
8:21	29:4; 44:5,6
9:1	59:8
11:4	33:14

Genesis *(Gen, Gn) cont'd:*

13:2	70:9
13:14	70:5
17:5	15:1
17:15	15:1
18:3	77:5
18:21	85:8
18:27	16:2; 71:5,6
19:1	5:2
22:8	76:7
22:12	45:3
24:53	77:1
27:1-40	21:7
27:9	71:4
27:11	28:2
27:22	28:3,7
27:23	28:2; 71:13
27:27	30:3; 47:3; 60:8
27:28	30:2; 54:5; 84:5
28:16	61:4
28:17	23:13
29:16-29	41:5
29:17	40:1
29:17-31	9:8
29:31	46:5
31:5	74:7
32:1	5:2
32:2	39:4
32:12	66:9
32:26	79:4
32:30	33:6; 45:6
37:27	2:6; 26:7
38:26	38:4
39:2	71:12
39:6	40:1
39:9	13:4
40:7	9:1
42:7	12:4
43:29	71:6
43:30	12:4

Indexes prepared by Tobias Meeker OCSO

ABBREVIATIONS

CCSL	*Corpus Christianorum Series Latina.* Turnhout, Belgium. 1953-.
CF	Cistercian Fathers Series
Dil	Bernard of Clairvaux, *De diligendo Deo (On Loving God)*
D Sp	Dictionnaire de Spiritualité. Paris, 1932f
Gra	Bernard of Clairvaux, *De gratia et libero arbitrio (On Grace and Free Choice)*
	J. P. Migne, Patrologiae cursus completus, series latina. Rpt. Paris, 1957–64.
RB	*Regula monachorum sancti Benedicti (Rule of St Benedict)*
SBOp	Sancti Bernardi Opera, edd. J. Leclercq, H. M. Rochais, C. H. Talbot. Rome, 1957–
SC	Bernard of Clairvaux, *Sermones super Cantica canticorum Sermons on the Song of Songs)*
Spec fid	William of St Thierry, *Speculum fidei (The Mirror of Faith)*

Psalms have been cited according to the Vulgate enumeration.